VALUE FOR MONEY IN PUBLIC–PRIVATE PARTNERSHIPS

AN INFRASTRUCTURE GOVERNANCE APPROACH

MARCH 2022

ASIAN DEVELOPMENT BANK

ADB

Contents

Tables, Figures, and Boxes

Foreword

The coronavirus disease (COVID-19) pandemic is far from over, and its effects are felt throughout Asia and the Pacific, especially for the lower-income countries. Planning, project preparation, and investment in resilient infrastructure will enhance preparedness for future pandemics and climate-related shocks in the new normal. The stimulative effect of infrastructure on economic growth, jobs, connectivity, and inclusivity is well established, but public financing and multilateral banks only account for about 45% of infrastructure needs. Public–private partnerships (PPPs) are part of the solution to narrow the financing gap by mobilizing private sector finance and efficiency. However, to avoid severe fiscal impacts that could damage investor perception, it is important that PPP infrastructure delivers on its promise to provide value for money.

Over the past 5 years, at a time when infrastructure PPPs can contribute to meeting this infrastructure investment challenge, the global level of PPP transactions in Asia and the Pacific has been declining. While the most recent decline is due to COVID-19, there is also concern on the government side that PPPs are not resulting in "value for money" as intended and, from a private sector perspective, that the risks associated with PPPs are excessive and do not provide needed flexibility. This publication reflects the essential role of the Asian Development Bank (ADB) as a knowledge solutions bank to help developing member countries tackle complex challenges. It provides a governance approach to promoting value for money to strengthen public sector capacity to prepare and implement PPP infrastructure investments. These investments need to be fiscally sustainable and bankable, to achieve their socioeconomic goals, and to be designed and implemented to be resilient to climate shocks and natural hazards.

ADB's support for sustainable infrastructure is in line with its Strategy 2030 operational priority of strengthening developing member country governance and institutional capacity. This publication supports the Group of 20 (G20) Principles for Quality Infrastructure Investment (QII), which aim to maximize the positive economic, social, and environmental impact of infrastructure; raise economic efficiency to deliver value for money; build resilience against disasters; and strengthen infrastructure governance while ensuring sound public finances.

As Asia and the Pacific deals with the lingering consequences of the pandemic, countries will look to the private sector in tandem with public finance to stimulate economic growth for a green, resilient, and inclusive recovery. It is urgent that developing countries ensure PPP investment plans maximize the economic impact of infrastructure investment, especially at a time of fiscal constraints and elevated national debts. This calls for an effective infrastructure governance approach to value for money to ensure performance over the asset life cycle and to maximize the quality and amount of infrastructure for a given level of spending.

Bruno Carrasco
Director General concurrently Chief Compliance Officer
Sustainable Development and Climate Change Department

Acknowledgments

This report is led by Hanif Rahemtulla, principal public management specialist, Governance Thematic Group of the Sustainable Development and Climate Change Department (SDTC-GOV); Joao Pedro Farinha, principal financial sector economist, Public Management, Financial Sector and Trade Division, Central and West Asia Department (CWPF); and Sanjay Grover, senior public–private partnership specialist, PPP-Thematic Group Secretariat (PPP-TGS) of the Asian Development Bank. The lead writers are Michael Schur, infrastructure finance specialist and David Bloomgarden, public investment management specialist.

The project team wishes to acknowledge the technical feedback provided by Adrian Torres, chief of PPP-TGS; Jamie Leather, chief of Transport Sector Group, Sector Advisory Service Cluster (SDSC-TRA); Srinivas Sampath, director, South Asia Department Urban Development and Water Division (SEUW); Ashish Narain, principal economist, Social Sectors and Public Sector Management Division, Pacific Department (PASP);

Hans van Rijn, principal public management specialist, Public Management, Financial Sector, and Regional Cooperation Division (EAPF); Olivier Leonard, principal procurement specialist, Financial Management Department (PFP1); Vivek Rao, principal financial sector specialist, Public Management, Financial Sector, and Regional Cooperation Division (SEPF); and Keerthi Kumar Challa, associate project officer (Energy), India Resident Mission.

We would also like to thank the following for their feedback on the case studies: Andrew Jeffries, country director, Vietnam Resident Mission; Kelly Bird, country director, Philippines Country Office; Said Zaidansyah, deputy country director, Indonesia Resident Mission (IRM); Jose Antonio Tan III, director, SEPF; Amr J. Qari, principal infrastructure specialist, IRM; Donald Lambert, principal private sector development specialist, VRM; and Stephen Schuster, principal financial sector specialist, SEPF.

Abbreviations

ADB	Asian Development Bank
COVID-19	coronavirus disease
DMC	developing member country
G20	Group of 20
GDP	gross domestic product
IMF	International Monetary Fund
IPSA	International Public Sector Accounting Standards
NPV	net present value
OECD	Organisation for Economic Co-operation and Development
PIMA	Public Investment Management Assessment
PPP	public–private partnership
PSC	public sector comparator
QII	Quality Infrastructure Investment
RCF	reference class forecasting
SBM	shadow bid model
SOE	state-owned enterprise
UK	United Kingdom
VFM	value for money

Executive Summary

This publication presents a governance perspective and approach to the application of value for money (VFM) considerations in the project-selection process and affordability analysis of public–private partnerships (PPPs). It begins with some background on the state of the PPP market and its relative decline over the past 5 years. This decline is contextualized by the severe economic disruption caused by the coronavirus disease (COVID-19) pandemic and its impact on the public debts and fiscal revenues of many countries. COVID-19 is likely to have reduced the public resources available for infrastructure investment.

The publication explains the rationale and value addition of a governance approach to VFM in infrastructure procurement is described in this technical note. It sets out how governments should make funding, procurement and investment decisions for infrastructure investments within a medium-term budget and fiscal framework. It provides a definition of VFM and outlines the key drivers that can deliver greater VFM relative to traditional public sector options for procuring infrastructure. These include risk transfer, whole-life costing, integration of capital investment with operations and maintenance under the responsibility of one party, budget certainty, innovation, asset utilization, accountability, and transparency.

Also discussed in this technical note is a governance model based on the International Monetary Fund (IMF) Public Investment Management Assessment (PIMA) framework. It shows that good project outcomes critically depend on the design and effectiveness of institutions that govern PPP planning, resource allocation, and project implementation. Accounting practices for PPPs do not create fiscal space. The International Public Sector Accounting Standards (IPSAS32) have, since 2014, required full recognition of the liabilities and assets created by PPP procurement on an accrual basis.

Further, this publication describes the standard methodologies for comparing PPPs with traditional public procurement options across the different stages of a project's development and for making the necessary adjustments for a fair comparison. It argues that a government's investment decision to implement and/or finance an infrastructure project should be separate from the decision to use a PPP model or traditional public option to procure the project. The sole reason for a PPP should be that it delivers superior VFM than traditional procurement, but international experience has shown that this objective is not an automatic outcome. Governments need to assess VFM throughout the procurement process, at the post-financial close, and over the project life cycle to verify that development results are in line with VFM expectations. This technical note provides Asian case studies and country examples to illustrate what good practice looks like and how to achieve it. In sum, the proposed governance approach is geared toward ensuring that fiscal sustainability and VFM in PPPs are not a random result, but are actively promoted by key public policy choices and project design decisions.

A robust governance approach ensures alignment with principle two of the Group of 20 (G20) Principles for Quality Infrastructure Investment (QII). This calls for assessing VFM in PPPs to raise economic efficiency based on whole-life costs, fiscal sustainability, affordability, risk assessment and allocation, and climate mitigation and resiliency. A sound governance framework also recognizes that VFM is not a guaranteed outcome from PPP procurement. Rather, it must be secured, not simply at a point in time, but over the entire project life cycle by targeting the intended socioeconomic and environmental benefits. This technical note sets out key governance conclusions for supporting VFM analysis in ADB developing member countries (DMCs) to ensure that PPPs, in suitable projects, deliver better outcomes than any alternative delivery model.

1. Introduction

Background: Recent Trends and Value for Money

At a time when PPPs can contribute to the financing and delivery of quality infrastructure, the global level of PPP transactions is declining. PPP investment in 2019 equalled $96.7 billion for a volume of 409 projects, a 3% decrease from 2018 investment levels of $99.7 billion. In 2019, PPP investment fell 7% short of the previous 5-year average of $103.5 billion but recovered from the 10-year low of $76.8 billion in 2016.[1] As of June 2020, East Asia and the Pacific

showed PPP commitments of $4.4 billion, a 79% decrease from June 2019; South Asia reported a 33% decrease compared to the first half of 2019.

The People's Republic of China leads the region in PPP commitments, with investments totalling $2.9 billion in the first half of 2020, the lowest level of the last 5 years.[2] While the coronavirus disease (COVID-19) pandemic undoubtedly impacted the PPP market, the trend over the past 5 years suggests a perception by policy-makers that new PPPs do not deliver "value for money" (VFM) as previously believed, and that past levels of adoption of PPP modalities were in excess of ideal or feasible limits.

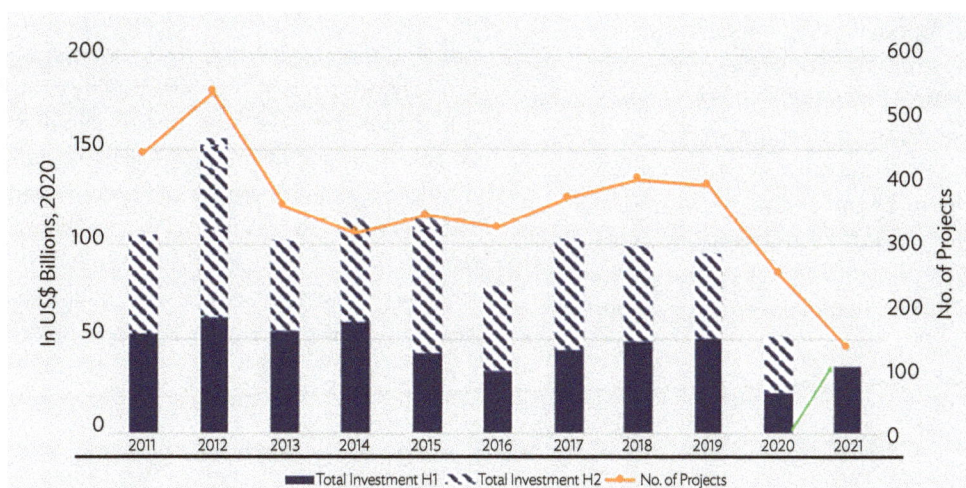

Figure 1: Investment Commitments in Infrastructure Projects with Private Participation in Emerging Market and Developing Economies, 2011–H1 2021

Source: World Bank, Private Participation in Infrastructure (PPI) Half Year Report, 2021. Countries covered are all developing member countries of the World Bank.

---

[1] World Bank. 2020. PPI Database.

[2] Data for the first half of 2020 comes from the PPI Database half-year report and is based on the World Bank regional classification the Asia Pacific. See https://ppi.worldbank.org/en/ppi.

The International Monetary Fund (IMF) projects a recovery in 2021–2022 with global growth of 5.9% in 2021 and 4.9% in 2022; however, divergent growth paths will create wider income inequality between advanced economies and developing economies. New pandemic variants and supply disruptions continue to pose risks to growth projections.[3] As part of the COVID-19 recovery, countries will turn to infrastructure to stimulate economic growth at a time when they face fiscal constraints and elevated national debts. The imperative for careful project prioritization and selection is driven by the most rapid and broad-based debt increase in emerging markets and developing economies in the past 50 years. Since 2010, total debt among developing countries increased by 60% of gross domestic product (GDP) to a historic level of more than 170% of GDP in 2019.[4]

As a response to the economic impact of COVID-19, and to ensure access to sustainable infrastructure and infrastructure services, the Asian Development Bank (ADB) will further strengthen its support for improving DMCs' public sector capacity to prepare and implement both traditional infrastructure investments and PPPs that are fiscally sustainable and achieve their social and economic development objectives. This support is guided by ADB's *Strategy 2030* and aligned with the Principles for QII. These principles call for maximizing the positive impact of infrastructure investment while (i) ensuring sustainable public finances, (ii) increasing economic efficiency taking into account life-cycle costs, (iii) assessing social and environmental costs and women's economic empowerment, (iv) building resilience against disasters and climate change, and (v) adopting measures to improve infrastructure governance.[5] Infrastructure governance comprises the public institutions, processes, and procedures that guide government decisions in planning, allocating funds, and implementing public investment projects, including PPPs. To ensure the selection of the highest quality projects for sustainable and resilient infrastructure, VFM analysis can improve the overall quality of project preparation and risk management, especially fiscal risk management.

This technical note will contribute to ADB's PPP support in DMCs for upstream policy and regulation and midstream processes and procedures for project and portfolio decisions. This is guided by the *Public–Private Partnership Operational Plan 2012–2020*[6] and informed by a recent evaluation of *ADB Support for PPPs (2009–2019)*. The evaluation identified a need for ADB to provide stronger support to DMCs to improve their capacity to screen and select projects using VFM analysis, and to improve the quality of PPP project structuring and delivery.[7]

Rationale for a Governance Approach to Value for Money

A key value addition of this technical note is the presentation of a practical governance perspective on how to contextualize VFM in the project-selection process, and how it differs from cost–benefit analysis, project prioritization, and affordability analysis. The publication discusses how funding decisions should be guided by a medium-term fiscal and budget framework, while financing and procurement options should be guided by VFM.[8] DMC governments, development practitioners, and development partners can use this note as a reference in establishing decision-making processes to govern upstream stages

3   International Monetary Fund.2021. World Economic Outlook, Recovery During a Pandemic, Health Concerns, Supply Disrruptions, and Price Pressures. October.

4   Kose, M.A. et al. 2020. Caught by a Cresting Debt Wave; Global Waves of Debt: Causes and Consequences. Finance & Development. Volume 57. Washington, DC: World Bank.

5   Available at: https://www.mof.go.jp/english/international_policy/convention/g20/annex6_1.pdf. QII is an ambitious agenda set out by the G20 at the 2016 Hangzhou Summit and the 2019 Osaka Summit that produced the QII principles. The QII principles represent the G20's common strategic direction for infrastructure development. The QII principles highlight the importance of the quality of infrastructure investment as part of countries' national development strategies to close their infrastructure gaps.

6   ADB. 2012. *Public–Private Partnership Operational Plan 2012–2020*.

7   ADB. 2020. *ADB Support for Public–Private Partnerships 2009-2019*. Thematic evaluation.

8   The medium-term fiscal framework provides the fiscal parameters for the government's resource envelope over the medium term; the medium-term budget framework lays out the government's investments priorities within those agreed parameters. The term funding refers to how the government will pay for the cost of a project over time out of the budget or from user fees. This differs from financing which refers to the debt and equity used to cover costs up front for the construction of the project.

of project development. It will help them determine, for example, what projects are worth pursuing, what projects should be prioritized, what projects can be fiscally afforded, and how to best procure such projects. This is crucial to ensure that investment decisions are made independently of, and prior to, financing and procurement; and that they are required and transparently recorded by the DMCs' own governance frameworks of laws, regulations, and institutional processes. This technical note cites case studies and country examples to illustrate what good practice looks like and how to achieve it.

The publication outlines limitations of widely used VFM methodologies (see Section 3), which are mainly due to unreliable quantitative data and optimistic assumptions, and what some countries are doing to obtain more reliable outcomes from VFM analysis. It also highlights the importance of an infrastructure governance framework to systematically ensure the achievement of VFM in PPP projects. This needs to be applied not only at the bidding stage (i.e., ex-ante or potential VFM) but also over the entire project life cycle to ensure de facto VFM. This technical note describes how best to implement ex-post evaluations to determine if the project delivered VFM and to develop lessons learned for future projects. This requires a high level of capacity in government contracting authorities to plan, develop, procure, and manage infrastructure projects.

This publication note complements ADB's report on supporting quality infrastructure in DMCs[9] and will inform a PPP direction strategy paper currently in preparation. It draws from a recent *ADB Governance Brief* (2020) on restoring confidence in PPPs.[10] Other related documents include the ADB procurement guidance note on VFM in public sector projects[11] and ADB's *Guidelines for the Economic Analysis of Projects*.[12] In addition, there are several VFM publications by international organisations that present generalized global guidelines and principles. A bibliography of these sources is provided in Appendix 2 for reference and further research.

---

[9]   ADB. 2021. ADB Special Report – Supporting Quality Infrastructure in Developing Member Countries. Manila. This report analyzes the importance of quality infrastructure governance, focusing on better understanding the constraints countries face across the investment cycle and the inefficiencies that undermine the value addition proposition. The report identifies limited public investment management capacity as a constraint to reducing the infrastructure gap and ensuring the effective allocation of public resources to maximize the economic benefits of infrastructure investment.

[10] Mosely, M. 2020. Restoring Confidence in Public–Private Partnerships Reforming Risk Allocation and Creating More Collaborative PPPs. ADB. Manila. This paper examines several alternative contractual arrangements for infrastructure projects and proposes alternative risk allocations and their suitability for achieving VFM in PPPs following the COVID-19 pandemic.

[11] ADB. 2018. Value for Money Guidance Note on Procurement. The Guidance Note on Strategic Procurement Planning assists DMCs in developing procurement strategies and procurement plans for loan and grant projects financed by ADB. Both the ADB guidance note on VFM as applied to PPPs requires an evaluation of costs and benefits along with all relevant risks, nonprice attributes, and the total cost of ownership of an asset. The key difference is that the guidance note applies to traditional public sector procurement whereas VFM for PPPs compares traditional public sector procurement with PPP procurement to determine which delivers the best VFM.

[12] ADB. 2017. Guidelines for the Economic Analysis of Projects. According to these guidelines, an economically viable project should, first, embody the most efficient and least cost option to achieve the intended project outcomes. Second, the economic surplus should be above project opportunity cost. And third, operations and maintenance (O&M) should have sufficient funding to ensure fiscal, socioeconomic, and environmental sustainability in line with the project's objectives.

2. What is Value for Money?

Value for Money: A Definition

ADB defines VFM for PPPs as follows:

"Value for money (VFM) in public–private partnership (PPP) projects is gained through the engagement of private sector efficiency, effectiveness, and economy and through the appropriate allocation of risks in the project. The assessment of the potential to secure VFM is a key element of the PPP assessment process. The conclusions on VFM potential will inform governments in developing member countries (DMCs) on whether to proceed with a PPP procurement, and, if so, the form of PPP that could be used."[13]

VFM assesses whether the socioeconomic and development objectives are more effectively captured in the PPP arrangement relative to conventionally procured projects. Undertaking this assessment is often easier said than done. Many developing countries lack defined methodologies to undertake the fiscal affordability and risk analyses that go into determining the VMF.[14] Benefits are often overestimated and costs underestimated, resulting in a failure to adequately consider alternatives during VFM analysis. This leads procuring authorities to overstate VFM and to conclude that traditional procurement is a poor alternative.[15] On the other hand, PPPs can deliver VFM given adequate assessment of project risks, costs, and private sector capacity to improve the efficiency of the project relative to traditional public investment.

Value Drivers for Achieving Value for Money

In essence, VFM is achieved by harnessing private sector incentives for performance. Table 1 provides key value drivers and practical questions to assess whether a PPP can deliver VFM. The entries in the table form the basis for a qualitative VFM analysis.

---

[13] ADB. 2012. *Public–Private Partnership Operational Plan 2012–2020.* Appendix 3. While this definition is for PPPs, the ADB definition for sovereign lending VFM "enables the borrower to obtain optimal benefits through effective, efficient, and economic use of resources by applying, as appropriate, the core procurement principles and related considerations, which may include life-cycle costs and socioeconomic and environmental development objectives of the borrower. Price alone may not sufficiently represent VFM." The main difference with VFM for PPPs is that there is no decision between a public procurement and a PPP. See ADB. *Value for Money: Guidance Note on Procurement, 2018.*

[14] World Bank Group. 2020. *Benchmarking Infrastructure Development 2020: Assessing Regulatory Quality to Prepare, Procure, and Manage PPPs and Traditional Public Investment in Infrastructure Projects.* World Bank, Washington, DC.

[15] World Bank Group. 2017. *Public–Private Partnerships Reference Guide.* Version 3, p. 24. Washington, DC.

Table 1:   Value Drivers for Value for Money

Value Driver	Value for Money Assessment Questions
Risk transfer	Are risks appropriately priced and allocated to the party who is best able to manage and mitigate risks at the lowest cost? Can competitive tension be ensured when risk pricing and allocation are embedded in a contractual obligation?
Life-cycle costing	Is one party responsible for construction, operations and maintenance, and renewal costs over the life of the asset? Is the asset being procured factored in the overall cost of construction, operations, and maintenance?
Budget certainty	Is there a contractual commitment upfront to ensure life-cycle costs of the project? Is this cost incorporated into the medium-term fiscal and budget frameworks?
Service delivery	Is there a long-term performance-based contract to deliver service when and as required?
Innovation	Is there a competitive bidding process that encourages bidders to develop innovative solutions based on output specifications?
Multiple asset streams	Are private parties incentivized to use a special purpose single facility to focus on project deliverables and support multiple revenue streams (i.e., user fees) that offset costs?
Accountability and performance	Do payments from the government depend on the performance of the contractor to deliver service on time, on budget, and in line with output specifications? Does the government have the institutional mechanisms to effectively monitor performance and exercise the necessary scrutiny to uphold contractual obligations?
Transparency and consultation	Has there been an effective process of consultation and information sharing with stakeholders (market players, related public sector entities, and civil society) to mitigate social, economic, and political influence risks? Has (can) procurement governance ensured (ensure) competitive tension at bidding?

Source: Authors.

Value for Money Should Be the Key Driver of Public–Private Partnership Procurement

VFM analysis needs to recognize that VFM should be the key driver of PPP procurement, not any notion of fiscal space or perceived fiscal constraints. This is because PPPs do not create fiscal space, as often perceived by decision-makers (and commonly articulated by some stakeholders). There is no intrinsic difference in the fiscal impact of a PPP versus conventional government procurement. A PPP creates liabilities for the government in three ways: (i) through the present value of a future commitment to pay for the service, for example, the present value of a series of availability payments; (ii) through the creation of

contingent liabilities, for example, the obligation to make termination payments under certain conditions; and (iii) through foregone revenue, which the government could have collected and booked as recurrent revenue in its budget, if a user-payer model is a key part of the PPP concession.

The value of the liability created by PPP procurement is the same as the liabilities created through conventional procurement. The government, first and foremost, must establish that it has funds to pay for a project. Only after establishing that should it consider whether PPP procurement offers VFM. While PPPs may change the financing and delivery of an infrastructure asset, they do not change the funding responsibility, which ultimately resides with taxpayers and/or users. Responsibility for the costs of PPPs is ultimately borne by government fiscal authorities, in which case the government foregoes a new revenue stream in favor of the PPP concessionaire. The initial capital cost is often financed wholly or in part by the private sector under a PPP project. Fiscal authorities, however, still pay the cost of a PPP project, but it is spread out over time through availability payments or contingent liabilities.

Both conventionally procured projects and PPPs can offset project costs (capital, finance, and operations) with user revenues. The degree to which this is possible should really make no difference to either procurement method. Any gap between user revenue and project costs can only be funded by government fiscal authorities (ultimately by taxpayers).

Thus, the logic that PPPs do not change the funding obligation of governments holds true regardless of the PPP model. Take, for example, a privately financed expressway project, funded in one of the following two ways:

(i)   by taxpayers (i.e., an availability payment PPP): any budget savings during construction must be offset by subsequent payments to the PPP company that allows it to recover the costs of construction, finance, and operation of the asset; or

(ii)   by users (i.e., a toll revenue PPP): the ability of governments temporarily to avoid the upfront investment is equivalent, in net present value terms, to any expressway toll revenue foregone by government during operation.

PPPs also do not generally change project risks. These are the same regardless of how a project is procured. PPPs change how risks are allocated and managed, but not the underlying risks themselves. What PPPs do is to add a new layer of medium- and long-term financial risks that are connected to the obligations embedded in the concession. The basis of VFM in PPP projects is thus the ability to transfer certain project risks to a private party that can more effectively manage such risks at a lower cost. Since PPPs do not

change funding obligations, VFM must be a key reason to embark on PPPs.

Under conventional procurement, the government has an obligation to service the project debt that it issued (or the liabilities it contracted) to resource the project. Under PPP procurement, the government might have an obligation to make future payments if it foregoes the revenue stream from the infrastructure service in favor of the concessionaire or take into account future contingent liabilities such as termination payouts.

Since 2014, the International Public Sector Accounting Standards (IPSAS32) have required the full recognition of the liabilities and assets created by PPP procurement.[16] Many countries globally, as well as international organisations such as the Association of Southeast Asian Nations (ASEAN) and the Organisation for Economic Co-operation and Development (OECD), have committed to adopting IPSAS, but take-up in Asia has progressed slowly.[17]

Regarding the recognition of an asset, IPSAS32 states:

> *Para. 9: The grantor shall recognize an asset provided by the operator and an upgrade to an existing asset of the grantor as a service concession asset if:*
>
> *(a)   The grantor controls or regulates what services the operator must provide with the asset, to whom it must provide them, and at what price.*
>
> *(b)   The grantor controls—through ownership, beneficial entitlement or otherwise—any significant residual interest in the asset at the end of the term of the arrangement.*

Regarding the recognition of a liability, IPSAS32 states:

> *Para. 14: Where the grantor recognizes a service concession asset in accordance with paragraph 9, the grantor shall also recognize a liability.*

---

16   See https://www.ifac.org/system/files/publications/files/B8%20IPSAS_32.pdf.

17   Wang, Z and Miraj, J. 2018. Adoption of International Public Sector Accounting Standards in Public Sector of Developing Economies – Analysis of Five South Asian Countries. *Research in World Economy*. This article points out challenges to the adoption of IPSAS due to lack of experienced staff, delays in provision of information by other government agencies, and lack of a defined timeframe. Countries reviewed in this study include India, Nepal, Bangladesh, Pakistan, and Sri Lanka.

Para. 15: *The liability recognized in accordance with paragraph 14 shall be initially measured at the same amount as the service concession asset measured in accordance with paragraph 11, adjusted by the amount of any other consideration (e.g., cash) from the grantor to the operator, or from the operator to the grantor.*

Adherence to the accounting standards will largely eliminate the belief of decision-makers that PPPs create fiscal space (or lift fiscal constraints) and will focus the procurement decision solely on VFM.

Investment and Procurement Decisions

Government must distinguish between an investment decision and a procurement decision. The investment decision refers to an assessment to determine if the infrastructure project delivers socioeconomic and environmental outputs that implement government policies and development objectives, regardless of the modality of procurement. A procurement decision refers to how the project is procured—whether it is a PPP or traditional public procurement. Australia, for example, ensures the distinction between investment and procurement decision through a budget rule. The budget rule requires that an investment decision on the social and economic benefits of the project comes before the procurement decision (see Box 1).

Best practice typically requires that all potential capital investments be subjected to rigorous economic appraisal, and that those deemed to have economic merit be ranked and funded within the fiscal constraints of the country's medium-term budget and fiscal framework. A project with a positive cost–benefit analysis should be a candidate for inclusion in the list of projects to be a candidate for implementation. Affordability analysis, based on the life-cycle cost of current and future projects, is then used to help determine priorities. Its goal is to avoid starting new projects that cannot be accommodated within the reasonable expectations for future fiscal resources.

This budget rule ensures that prioritization is not swayed by the ways in which projects may be procured (i.e., financed and delivered). The subsequent procurement decision is then an assessment of which delivery method will more likely ensure that the project objectives will be achieved. While this is determined by VFM tests, it only makes sense if the project is worth investment in the first place, which is something determined by a cost–benefit analysis and other prioritization tests.

PPPs are often perceived as creating fiscal space based on how they are accounted for in the public budget accounts. In cash accounting, the implementation of a PPP defers recognition of liability until after the asset is fully constructed. For large, complex assets, this may be as long as 4–5 years. This deferment could provide countries facing deficit or debt constraints with perverse incentives to pursue PPPs. Public pressure over fiscal deficits or public debt constraints often incentivizes governments to implement a PPP independently of whether or not a PPP delivers better VFM compared to traditional procurement. Mongolia experienced this in its first adoption of the PPP model for the road sector (see Box 2) as did many OECD countries. This situation reveals the consequences of not having established a process equivalent to the budget rule.

Box 1: Case Study: The Budget Rule in Australia

There is no legislative framework or overall set of rules governing public–private partnerships (PPPs) in Australia. Decisions on project-selection and procurement method are the responsibility of "line agencies," while control over funds rests within each Treasury. In New South Wales (NSW), Australia's largest state, the Public Authorities (Financial Arrangements) Act of 1987 (PAFA) asserts this control, allowing a line agency to enter into a joint financing arrangement such as a PPP only with the Treasurer's approval.

The federal government shares funding responsibilities with state governments for many infrastructure sectors. The states, however, bear a high proportion of the funding obligation and almost all the delivery responsibility for urban roads, ports, electricity supply, public transport, water and sewerage systems, education, health facilities, and public housing.

Strong governance processes across project planning, preparation and implementation stages are key to achieving value for money (VFM) in PPP projects. NSW, for example, develops and updates every 5 years a rolling 20-year infrastructure plan. These plans include business cases for the projects with the highest priority over the first 5 years. Planning beyond 5 years considers economic trends and the long-term outlook for economic development in the state.

Project preparation is subject to comprehensive business planning, with all projects required to develop "problem definition," "strategic business case," and "detailed business case" reports prior to the funding decision, and then regular updates to the business case following the funding decision or after procurement. Most states in Australia adopt a "budget rule" as part of the project preparation process, prior to implementation. The budget rule separates the procurement and investment decisions in accordance with the following:

(i)   Investment Decision (Is the project worth doing?) The Treasury assesses cost–benefit analysis, business case, and/or affordability analysis and how the project fits strategic priorities of the government.

(ii)   Procurement Decision (What procurement method yields the greatest VFM?) The Treasury reviews value for money and analysis of how the project serves the public interest.

Line ministries prepare funding submissions for the investment decision to the Expenditure Review Committee (ERC) of Cabinet, with support from their detailed business plans. The ERC also receives gateway reports (independent reviews of project costs, benefits, and risks), and has an opportunity to consider whether the relevant line ministry has adopted the gateway review team's recommendations. NSW Treasury, Infrastructure NSW, and the Premier's Department separately provide advice to the ERC regarding the merits or otherwise of line ministry capital project funding requests. The ERC is the ultimate funding approval body for all capital projects. Funding approval always includes a provision for contingent risk at each stage of the project cycle from the strategic business case to project delivery. After the government makes the investment decision and prior to the procurement decision, the agency responsible for the project prepares a budget for the project in line with the capital budget. All projects compete for a budget, and funding is allocated according to the strategic priority for each project. This helps to ensure that the availability of funding does not determine the procurement decision, and the choice of procurement option—traditional public procurement or PPP—is based on what produces the best VFM. The default assumption is for traditional public procurement, but if it turns out that a PPP delivers the best VFM, the government adjusts the capital amortization schedule to provide funding over the life of the project.

Sources: INSW. 2018. Building Momentum. State Infrastructure Strategy. https://insw-sis.visualise.today/documents/INSW_2018SIS_BuildingMomentum.pdf; NSW. Infrastructure Statement. https://www.budget.nsw.gov.au/sites/default/files/budget-2019-06/Budget_Paper_2-Infrastructure%20Statement-Budget_201920.pdf.

Box 2: Case Study: Mongolia 2008 Build–Transfer Projects

In 2008, a Mongolian parliament resolution allowed build–transfer (BT) projects in the roads sector. Construction companies themselves financed the projects, usually through commercial borrowing that would be guaranteed and serviced by the Government of Mongolia. These schemes grew rapidly as neither the capital investment nor the loan liability was reflected in the budget or government financial statements—at least not until loan repayments came due. They increased from 3% of the total value of road projects in 2008 to more than 25% in 2009 and 2010.

As with all BT schemes, there was minimal or no transfer of risk to the private sector and no service delivery gain, so no possibility of value for money. The government simply used more expensive commercial borrowings to finance the projects as an alternative to less expensive government debt. The rural roads were overengineered and, thus, of high cost as the road agency had no budget responsibility for their costs—they were "off budget." Ultimately, the government cancelled several of these schemes as the fiscal costs grew, impacting investor confidence and setting back the government's public–private partnership (PPP) program. Drawing on those early, fiscally painful lessons, Mongolia promulgated the Law on Concessions, influenced by the United Nations Commission on International Trade Law (UNCITRAL) Model Legislative Provisions on Privately Financed Infrastructure Projects, in 2010.

The law allows the use of a wide variety of build–operate–transfer (BOT) models and other PPP models. It also provides a strong basis for contracting authorities to select concession projects, but not before carrying out a preliminary economic evaluation or feasibility study of the projects. Value for money (VFM) is expected to be enhanced by the requirement that the contracting authority must choose bidders through a competitive tender and a transparent, nondiscriminatory, and objective award procedure.

Since the law came into effect, the government has agreed to and executed several concession projects, and several others are in development. The government's PPP project list consists of more than 50 projects submitted by line ministries and five projects submitted by the private sector. Following a PPP involving the Mongolia Telecom Company in 1995, the country has entered into five additional PPPs, predominantly in the renewable energy sector. A total investment of $445 million has been committed to PPPs to date.

The European Bank for Reconstruction and Development (EBRD) has conducted several assessments on the effectiveness of legal frameworks governing PPP in the EBRD region. The EBRD rated compliance with the new law at 86 on a scale of 1-100. To support better implemention of the legal framework, Mongolia set up a PPP unit, which expanded the regulatory framework and has gained project experience since 2010. Further work is necessary, however, to improve preparation of the planned projects and ensure more transparent budget provisioning.

Source: 2017/2018 PPP Laws Assessment in the EBRD Region. European Bank for Reconstruction and Development, London. 2018.

3. Value for Money: The Need for a Governance-Based Approach

There is extensive literature on VFM as applied to PPP procurement. The literature typically covers best practice guidance, checklists, and practical techniques for undertaking both qualitative and quantitative VFM assessments (see Appendix 3). Most recently, the literature has paid attention to the practical difficulties of quantitative VFM assessments, generally focused on the inherent weaknesses of the mainstream approach, namely the development of a public sector comparator (PSC).

This technical note does not attempt to summarize this extensive literature on VFM and is generally in agreement with the key approaches, including the innovations around complementing measures such as the PSC. The key departure point in this note is to recognize that effective PPP governance is required to achieve VFM. In other words, regardless of the rigor with which the various VFM techniques, guidance, and analyses are applied, they will not be successful and VFM will not be achieved if the DMCs' overall PPP project governance framework is flawed or nonexistent.

Weaknesses in infrastructure governance exacerbate fiscal risks. Simply put, VFM analysis cannot mask deficiencies in the overall PPP project governance framework. The quality of public investment management frameworks varies among countries in the Asia and the Pacific, particularly in terms of appraisal and selection. In smaller island economies, there is usually no "competitive market" of potential bidders. In cases of weak infrastructure governance, PPPs may not be the best option and countries should consider alternative models. There is an array of alternative private participation structures in the region including concessions, leases, management contracts, and design–build–operate arrangements that may be more appropriate than PPPs under these circumstances.

This technical note has already shown that Mongolia's failure to embed its PPP program in a robust governance framework—in which PPPs were first screened for affordability and integrated with the medium-term budget and fiscal framework—meant it was impossible to achieve VFM from the first-round road PPP program. Moreover, even a project that demonstrates VFM is not necessarily affordable to the government. In the case of Mongolia, the program was simply not affordable within existing fiscal constraints. The fundamental breach of fiscal limits was a direct result of a flawed PPP governance framework that fell into the trap of "fiscal illusion" and a failure to recognize deferred liabilities for which the government was ultimately responsible.

PPP procurement is frequently shrouded in "fiscal illusions" that prevent careful fiscal risk management and allow for the approval and procurement of very costly or poorly structured projects. As mentioned above, there is a misperception that PPP procurement creates fiscal space that is otherwise constrained by a government's existing liabilities (direct and contingent). There are three main sources of fiscal illusion in PPPs. The first relates to accounting practices, asset recognition criteria, and fiscal risk assessment by public sector contracting agencies. By keeping PPPs off-budget, governments can increase long-term commitments in infrastructure without legislative scrutiny or oversight; this can jeopardize fiscal sustainability.[18] Accounting practices that allow governments to increase infrastructure without an immediate impact on public-sector deficits or debt are a large source of fiscal illusion. Second, fiscal illusion in PPPs can arise from a failure to recognize the implicit risks to a government of running PPPs as public infrastructure which may require unforeseen intervention (e.g., pretermination risks). Third, many fiscal risks in infrastructure originate from weaknesses in the early stages of the project cycle, mainly during strategic planning and project appraisal, resulting in inadequate assessment of the fiscal risks in PPP contracts.

Typical Value for Money Approaches

VFM analysis—as practiced almost everywhere and as described in most guidance on the topic, including in the examples cited in Appendix 3—typically involves a combination of qualitative and quantitative checks or tests, at specific points in time, to assess the PPP against the next best alternative.

Qualitative VFM analysis is a common-sense approach to determine if a PPP project is the best option for private sector financing and effective delivery of services. This analysis begins at the earliest stage of project screening to determine if the PPP can deliver VFM by considering the key drivers for private participation (Table 1). This includes the assessment of value drivers such as competitive tension, accountability, and performance-based contracting. A quantitative assessment often accompanies the quality VFM analysis when estimates can already be projected. It compares the PPP option against the option of traditional public procurement. Page 20 provides a description of this process; but, in general, it compares risk-adjusted fiscal costs for the public and

PPP options. There are alternative ways to make this comparison such as through a cost–benefit analysis, which quantitatively measures the benefits of the of traditional procurement against the benefits of a PPP. Whichever method is chosen, the analysis is done as part of project preparation and updated as a project moves from the procurement phase and more refined cost and technical data become available.

Value for Money Depends on the Strength of the Public–Private Partnership Project Governance Framework

The Organisation for Economic Co-operation and Development (OECD) defines the objective of the project governance framework as "... to ensure that infrastructure programmes make the right projects happen, in a cost-efficient and affordable manner, that is trusted by users and citizens to take their views into account." This refers to how governments manage their entire portfolio of infrastructure projects to select projects that have the greatest VFM in line with government policies and priorities. This helps governments to select the most viable projects for financing as either a PPP or a more traditional procurement. The OECD Council on the Governance of Infrastructure in July 2020 issued formal recommendations on infrastructure governance linking VFM to sustainability and affordability achieved through transparent and accountable capital budgeting, and rigorous procedures for project selection, appraisal, and risk allocation.[19] This proposed approach implies that it is crucial for the government to implement infrastructure governance in public investment management to (i) systematically produce VFM results and (ii) avoid ending up with a source of fiscal instability and inefficient public investment.

---

[18] See P. de Vries. Public Budget Norms and PPP, An Anomaly. https://www.taylorfrancis.com/chapters/edit/10.4324/9780203079942-24/public-budget-norms-ppp-anomaly-piet-de-vries; and Accountability and accounting for public–private partnerships. https://www.taylorfrancis.com/chapters/edit/10.4324/9780203079942-32/accountability-accounting-public–private-partnerships-ron-hodges?context=ubx&refId=5116a943-5b14-43f8-b835-ff563c666a57.

[19] See https://www.oecd.org/gov/infrastructure-governance/recommendation/. The OECD Council made 10 recommendations for the governance of infrastructure: (i) "adopt a long-term strategic vision for infrastructure; (ii) ensure fiscal sustainability and value for money; (iii) efficient procurement; (iv) stakeholder participation; (v) policy coordination across levels of government; (vi) predictable and efficient regulatory framework; (vii) whole-of-government approach to manage integrity risks; (viii) evidence informed decision-making; (ix) asset performance throughout its life; and (x) strengthen infrastructure resilience."

Effective PPP programs have adopted qualitative and quantitative approaches to the assessment of VFM. However, in the successful cases, VFM takes place within a robust PPP governance framework that assesses and focuses on securing VFM **at each and every step in the project cycle.** The argument that VFM must be earned at every step in the PPP project cycle has been made before—see, for example, Castalia (2016).[20]

This robust governance approach ensures that VFM is broadly aligned with principle two of QII, which calls for assessment of VFM for PPPs to raise economic efficiency based on life-cycle costs, fiscal sustainability, affordability, and risk assessment, allocation, and mitigation. A sound governance framework recognizes that VFM is not a guaranteed outcome from PPP procurement. Rather, it must be secured, not at a point in time, but over the entire project development life cycle and beyond, over the asset life cycle. It is crucial to emphasize that ex-ante expectations of VFM at financial closure can be defeated by difficulties during the construction phase, weak contract management and monitoring during implementation, or lack of proper (sector) regulatory oversight. The renegotiation of many PPPs that can undermine VFM can also be traced back to fundamental (but easily avoidable) flaws in the project development stage, which an effective governance framework would have rooted out.[21]

To illustrate the point, a sound governance framework for project development, which must be embedded in the legal and regulatory framework, recognizes that:

(i)   Even if (ex-ante, expected) VFM is demonstrated conceptually at the project-selection stage, as part of the procurement decision, there is no guarantee it will flow through to the project development stage.

(ii)   And even if VFM is reflected in the risk allocation embedded in the draft PPP contract during the development stage, there is no

guarantee it will not be negotiated out by the successful bidder at the tendering stage. In fact, this outcome is quite likely in the absence of competitive tension or when the public contracting party has not invested enough due diligence in its own contract drafting.

(iii)   And even if (ex-ante) VFM is secured in negotiations with the successful bidder at the tendering stage, there is no guarantee the government will administer the PPP contract in a way that maintains pressure for VFM during the implementation stage. The complexity and long-term nature of PPP contracts can result in incomplete contractual clauses due to pressure for an early and speedy approval process.

(iv)   And even if the government manages to ensure VFM during the implementation stage, there is no guarantee that the private concessionaire will be able to comply with terms of the original contract during actual operations, or that the government will administer the PPP contract in a way that secures VFM during the operations stage. These factors can contribute to renegotiation problems in PPPs caused by low-balling and strategic bidding by the private partners during the bidding and negotiation stage. The bidders know that their bargaining power increases during the implementation stage and can use it to force a renegotiation of the contract in their favor.[22] When low-balling and strategic bidding exposes the private partner to risks it cannot manage, the public partner will need to shoulder a significant financial burden to ensure uninterrupted public service.

(v)   Finally, there is no guarantee that VFM will be secured on future PPP projects unless those lessons are captured systematically as part of an independent, post-completion audit that assesses overall VFM relative to that determined during the initial procurement

20   Castalia, 2016. *Municipality-Level Public-Private Partnership (PPP) Operational Framework for Chongqing.* Consultant report to ADB: PPP Value for Money Guidance Note.

21   See https://blogs.worldbank.org/ppps/preventing-renegotiation-fostering-efficiency. Also, see an earlier OECD report: http://www.internationaltransportforum.org/jtrc/DiscussionPapers/DP201425.pdf.

22   E. Engel, R. Fischer, and A. Galetovic. 2019. Soft budgets and renegotiations in transport PPPs: An equilibrium analysis. *Economics of Transportation.* pp. 17, 40–50; E. Engel, R. Fischer, and A. Galetovic. 2015. Soft Budgets and Renegotiations in Public-Private Partnerships: Theory and Evidence. *Working Papers wp408.* University of Chile, Department of Economics.

decision. Thus, while VFM tests are often mentioned as a key element of due diligence in project development, VFM tests and VFM as a guiding principle cannot exist in isolation, and needs to be embedded in a robust governance framework to be relevant. Conversely, a robust governance framework requires VFM analysis to meet its objectives.

Infrastructure Governance and the International Monetary Fund Public Investment Management Assessment Framework

In a study of 17 OECD countries, the IMF found that increasing public investment can contribute to GDP growth through different mechanisms. On average, an increase of 1% of GDP in investment spending increases GDP by 0.4% in the same year. After 4 years, this same investment leads to a 1.5% increase in GDP, corresponding to a medium-term fiscal multiplier of about 1.4.[23] The study noted that these macroeconomic effects are almost four times stronger in countries with greater levels of public investment efficiency, in both the short and the medium term. In other words, "investing in investment," or public investment governance, matters to project aggregate outcomes. The effect of public investment in low-income countries tends to be shorter in duration and weaker than in advanced and middle-income economies.[24]

To measure country infrastructure governance capability, the IMF developed the Public Investment Management Assessment (PIMA) Framework, as in Figure 2. This evaluates infrastructure governance using 15 institutions that cover the three stages of the public investment cycle: planning, allocation, and implementation. The assessment is from three perspectives:

(i)   Institutional design: Are formal institutional requirements in place and are their roles in accordance with "good international practice?"

(ii)   Effectiveness (de facto): Are institutions performing adequately?

(iii)   Reform priority: What should be a country's reform priorities across the various public investment institutions?

The PIMA framework applies equally to PPP procurement, suggesting that good project outcomes, as reflected in VFM, depend critically on both the design and effectiveness of institutions that govern PPP planning, allocation, and implementation. The IMF has released aggregate data for the 14 countries[25] in Asia and the Pacific where PIMA assessments have been carried out. Figure 3 shows that the design of institutions and policies is often better than the actual implementation of policies. The light blue portions refer to the design of policies and the dark blue portions show the effectiveness with which the policies are implemented.

The least effective public investment management institutions in ADB's DMCs are those involved in appraising and selecting projects, maintenance funding, multiyear budgeting, and monitoring of public assets. Not only is design strength already low, but effectiveness in implementation is even lower.

These results have profound implications for achieving VFM in PPP procurement. ADB's *Public–Private Partnerships Monitor (Second Edition, 2019)* shows similar findings to the PIMA. According to the monitor, the "capacity of the public sector to plan, prepare, and procure PPP projects is inconsistent in all DMCs." The report states that often, there is little or no methodology behind the development of PPP pipelines and limited understanding in the public sector of PPP project selection and prioritization. Moreover, only 5 of 12 DMCs studied have guidance on risk allocation criteria, and PPP procurement

---

[23]   IMF. 2015. The Macroeconomic Effects of Public Investment: Evidence from Advanced Economies. *IMF Working Paper.*

[24]   Schwartz, G., et al. Well Spent: *How Strong Infrastructure Governance Can End Waste in Public Investment.* Washington, DC: International Monetary Fund.

[25]   Country PIMAs have been done in the following countries: Bangladesh, Bhutan, Cambodia, Indonesia, Kiribati, Malaysia, Maldives, Mongolia, Myanmar, the Philippines, Sri Lanka, Thailand, Timor-Leste, and Viet Nam.

is "insufficiently regulated" in 8 of the 12 DMCs.[26] Areas where implemenation effectiveness of public investment needs to be improved (see Figure 3) include the following:

(i) **Project Appraisal.** Weak project appraisal processes suggest that projects are not always selected based on VFM, and less likely to be so if they are to be procured as PPPs.

(ii) **Project Selection.** The IMF reports that most countries do not have an effective review of major projects by a central agency before inclusion in the budget. By implication, this means that there are deficiencies in the investment decision process, making a procurement decision based on VFM analysis less likely.

(iii) **Maintenance Funding.** Weaknesses in this area suggest that "whole of life cycle" costing is not undertaken, and projects may be constructed without appropriate budget allocations for maintenance. This is likely to lead to a bias toward PPP procurement, regardless of VFM, where maintenance funding is "guaranteed" by default through PPP procurement.

(iv) **Multiyear Budgeting.** Without forward budget estimates, again there will be a tendency to favor PPP procurement regardless of VFM as forward funding is "guaranteed" by default for such projects.

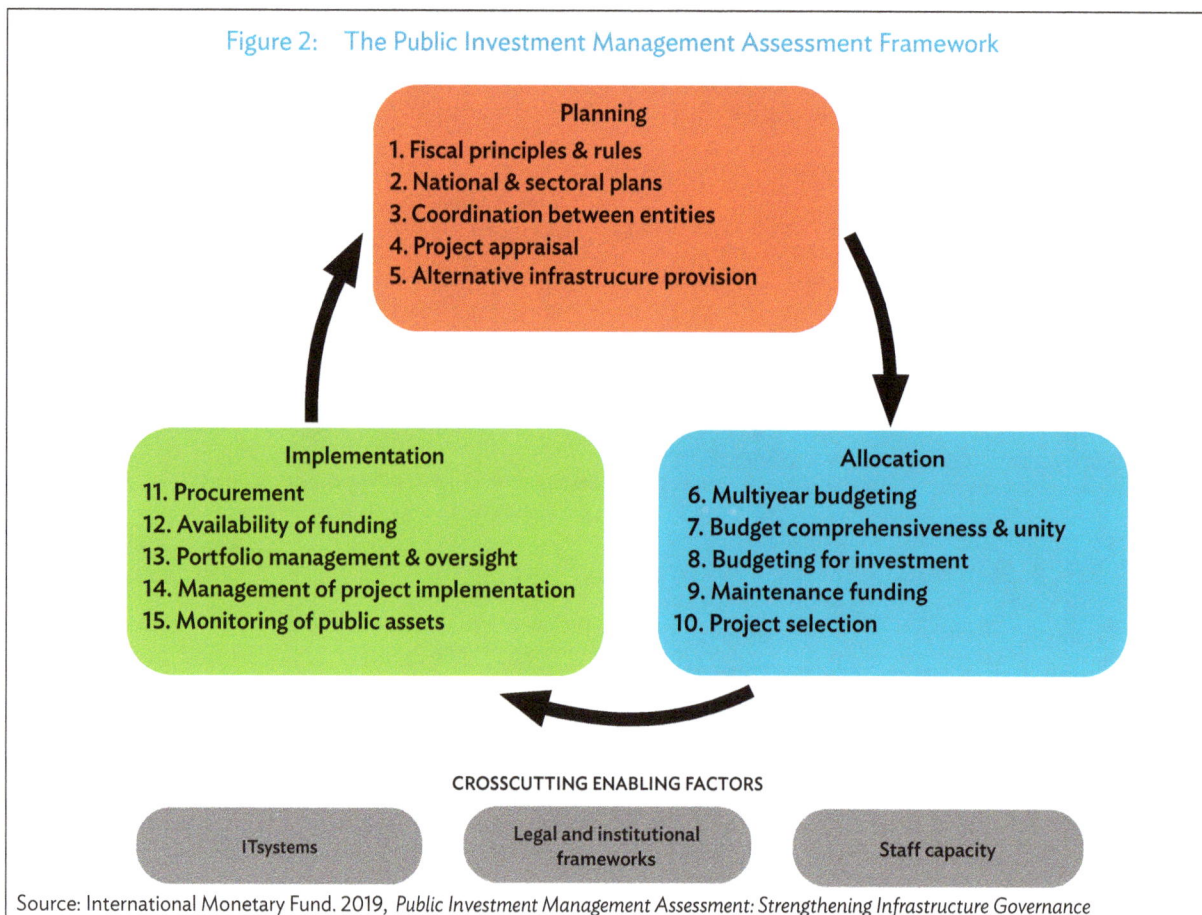

Figure 2: The Public Investment Management Assessment Framework

Planning
1. Fiscal principles & rules
2. National & sectoral plans
3. Coordination between entities
4. Project appraisal
5. Alternative infrastrucure provision

Implementation
11. Procurement
12. Availability of funding
13. Portfolio management & oversight
14. Management of project implementation
15. Monitoring of public assets

Allocation
6. Multiyear budgeting
7. Budget comprehensiveness & unity
8. Budgeting for investment
9. Maintenance funding
10. Project selection

CROSSCUTTING ENABLING FACTORS

ITsystems

Legal and institutional frameworks

Staff capacity

Source: International Monetary Fund. 2019, *Public Investment Management Assessment: Strengthening Infrastructure Governance*

---

[26] ADB. 2019. *Public–Private Partnership Monitor (Second Edition)*. p. xxii. Countries analyzed in this study are Bangladesh, Georgia, India, Indonesia, Kazakhstan, Papua New Guinea, Pakistan, the People's Republic of China, the Philippines, Sri Lanka, Thailand, and Viet Nam.

Figure 3:   Institutional Design and Effectiveness in Emerging and Developing Asia

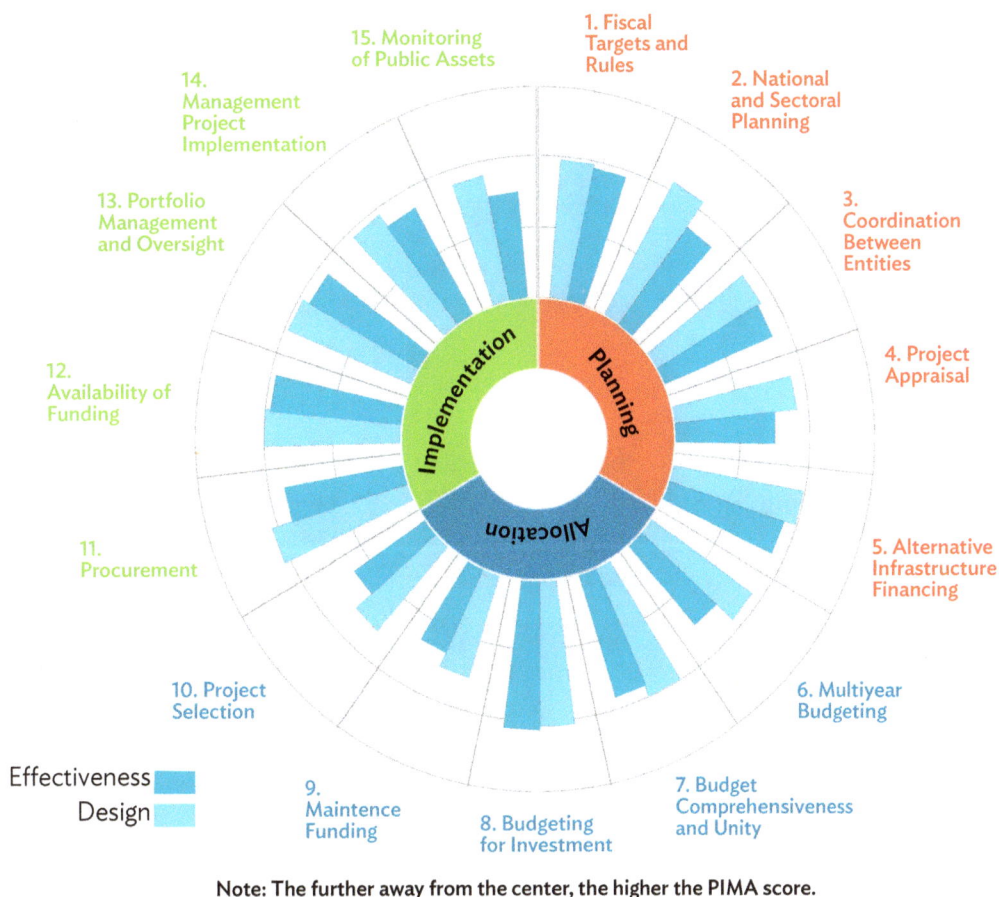

Note: The further away from the center, the higher the PIMA score.

PIMA = Public Investment Management Assessment.
Source: International Monetary Fund. Infrastructure Governance. Region: Asia & Pacific.

Value for Money and the Public–Private Partnership Project Cycle

VFM analysis should occur early in the project cycle and be updated throughout the project cycle based on a system of gateway checks and approval processes. Even at the stage of project implementation, revisiting the VFM analysis can confirm whether objectives are being realized and provide lessons for the procurement of future projects.

A trade-off exists between VFM analysis early in the project cycle when information is limited, and in later stages, when it is more difficult to make changes as the project gains momentum and support from politicians and other stakeholders is already crystallized.[27] Therefore, it is advisable to use an iterative approach with qualitative assessment predominating early in the project cycle, and quantitative assessment in later stages as more detailed and accurate information becomes available.

---

27   ADB, EBRD, IDB, IsDB, and WBG. 2016. *The APMG Public–Private Partnership (PPP) Certification Guide.* Washington, DC: World Bank Group. Chapter 4 of this publication provides a step-by-step description of each stage of the value for money assessment from appraisal to contract management.

A template framework is described in Table 2. The table describes stages of the approval process, what should be approved, and the required studies to provide evidence of the project's viability as a PPP. The table includes the typical types of entities responsible for each stage of approval; institutional set-ups vary according to national legal and regulatory environments.

Table 2:   Good Practice PPP Approval Process and Evidence

Stage	Approval	Evidence
Planning Ministry of Planning, Economy, and/or inter-agency entity		
Inclusion in long-term strategic planning	Approval of long-term infrastructure plan	High-level assessment of need
Project scoping	Approval of scoping studies for project	Confirmation of need and options analysis
Selection Ministry of Planning, Economy, inter-agency entity, and/or central budget authority		
Investment decision	Inclusion in the annual budget	Business case, including a cost–benefit analysis
Procurement decision	Approval to procure as a PPP	Preliminary VFM analysis, both qualitative and quantitative, and risk allocation
Procurement PPP unit, sector agency, SOE		
Project development	Approval to invite expression of interest (EOI)	Updated business case, further VFM analysis and risk allocation Draft contract prepared to match risk allocation
Expression of interest	Approval to issue request for proposals (RFP)	Updated business case, VFM analysis, risk allocation including market soundings analysis
Request for proposals	Approval of preferred bidder	Updated risk allocation, draft contract and VFM analysis
Negotiation and contract finalization	Approval for contract execution	Final VFM analysis based on final risk allocation Final contract terms and conditions Legal analysis that government has appropriate powers and rights to perform obligations specified in contract Institutional analysis that contract can be monitored and managed
Implementation Sector agency, SOE		
Management and monitoring	N/A	Performance is measured against key performance indicators
Completion Sector agency, SOE, Supreme Audit Institutions		
Ex-post evaluation at regular intervals	N/A	Project outcomes are compared to forecasts made during project development

N/A = not applicable, PPP = public–private partnership, SOE = state-owned enterprise, VFM = value for money.
Source: Authors.

A governance framework for VFM requires formal government approval, preferably at the highest possible level (e.g., ministerial), at key decision points in the process, to ensure that only projects that provide VFM make it to the tendering stage. Central agency control and management of the PPP governance process is key. This allows for projects that do not provide VFM to be eliminated early in the project cycle before the government expends considerable time, effort, and resources. At each decision point, the government reviews information to certify that a PPP continues to be the most suitable procurement option.

Securing Value for Money during Project Selection

Under a robust PPP project governance framework, projects considered for selection derive from long-term infrastructure plans and have previously been assessed for need and initial scoping, independent of the procurement method. This is crucial to avoid a myriad of problems that apply renegotiation pressures during the implementation of PPP concessions.[28] During the project-selection stage, projects in which benefits exceed costs are deemed worth pursuing. All projects that meet this objective are then prioritized, funded subject to fiscal constraints, and integrated with the medium-term budget and fiscal frameworks. This is the "investment decision." Projects that are fully funded in this way are now eligible to be considered for finance and implementation.

Some countries in Asia and the Pacific, including Cambodia, Fiji, Pakistan, the Philippines, and Thailand, have plans that set out their infrastructure challenges and opportunities, the government's planned projects, and areas of focus in terms of infrastructure investment and reform.[29] Once a decision is made that a project will enable a government to achieve its infrastructure objectives within fiscal constraints, a decision can be taken about the best procurement method to achieve VFM. However, most countries do not have whole-of-government planning, and those that do, including the ones cited here, may not consistently implement this type of planning or consistently determine the fiscal requirements required to accommodate priority projects. This is a crucial missing piece of the necessary governance framework, and it should be in place before PPP programs can be scaled-up.

During project selection, the government begins with a mainly qualitative assessment to determine if the proposed investment would be suitable for private sector financing and if the project is likely to achieve VFM. Four factors must be present for a PPP to be likely to offer VFM over other forms of procurement. Thus, a qualitative VFM assessment should focus on the initial assessment of these factors (see Appendix 1 or a more comprehensive set of qualitative considerations).

(i)   Is there a competitive market of potential bidders with the capability to undertake the project?

(ii) Can an efficient contract be written—that is, a contract that allows rights and obligations to be specified to provide a reasonable basis for valuation of the service to be provided?

(iii) Can performance of the service be objectively monitored and measured? This question should not only assess the relative complexities of the specific infrastructure service in question, but also ask hard questions about the regulatory oversight capacity in government to monitor contract implementation.

(iv) Can robust incentives be established that align with the government's and the private party's obligations under the PPP?

---

[28]   See OECD. 2020. Recommendation of the Council on the Governance of Infrastructure. Recommendation 1 calls for development of long-term vision for infrastructure informed by an assessment of current and future infrastructure needs. OECD also surveyed 27 OECD countries and highlighted the importance of a long-term infrastructure strategy to address infrastructure needs; the strategy should be politically sanctioned and coordinated across levels of government and the public. The study finds that Insufficient planning often impedes implementation and operation later in the project cycle. See *Getting Infrastructure Right: A framework for better governance.* Paris: OECD Publishing, https://doi.org/10.1787/9789264272453-en.

[29]   Global Infrastructure Hub. 2020. InfraCompass.

These four factors combine to make PPPs more likely to improve infrastructure delivery than other forms of procurement.

Competition

There must be enough bidders that have the expertise and experience to provide the service to the standard required and, importantly, they must be willing to do so. This highlights the importance of the "market sounding" phase of PPP procurement. Using the private sector in this way means there is "competition for the market" as it is unlikely there will be competition in the market for many public infrastructure projects.

The benefits of competitive provision will flow to the government or, more correctly, the users of the service. This competitive process helps assure VFM as the government can be confident that the price offered is the lowest practical price for delivery of the service. For many forms of infrastructure such as toll roads, airports, power stations, urban transit systems, and the like, there is competition; many private sector firms in many jurisdictions and internationally specialize in the life-cycle delivery of these services. Other areas such as health and education may have fewer firms with PPP experience, especially at the local level. Overall, the competitive PPP procurement process in many countries still needs to improve. According to the World Bank's *Benchmarking Infrastructure Development 2020*, the average rating for competitive PPP procurement practices in East Asia and the Pacific is 52 out of 100, compared to high-income OECD countries that score an average of 63 out of 100.[30]

Incomplete Contracts

A complete contract is one where the parties can specify their respective rights and obligations for every possible future state of the world. This means that both parties can value their roles under the contract efficiently and with certainty. Importantly, a complete contract ensures that all project risks can be defined and allocated to the party best able to either mitigate or manage them. Without a complete contract, efficient risk allocation cannot occur.

In practice, no contracts are complete. Thus, contracts contain dispute resolution processes, termination provisions, and ultimately the option of reverting to the courts to provide a degree of certainty. While such provisions can "fill the gaps" in any contract, efficient allocation and valuation of risks is obviously difficult where risks cannot be defined. The difficulty in developing complete contracts shows a PPP for a toll road is more likely to offer VFM than one for the provision of medical specialist services, which involves a high degree of technological obsolescence over time. For a toll road, the service to be offered over the life of the asset is reasonably well defined and, thus, reasonably certain obligations can flow from the contract. This is not the case for medical services. This is one reason why international experience has often resulted in policy advice for governments with weak infrastructure governance, such as conflict-affected countries, to refrain from entering certain, more complex subsectors when it comes to initiating PPP programs, so that the public sector can develop its own capacity first through experience and efforts to enhance regulatory credibility. For such countries with varying degrees of institutional capacity, various forms of private sector participation can be used that have lower capital requirements and shorter time horizons. These include management contracts, lease contracts, and O&M contracts.[31]

Measurable Service Standards

For a PPP to offer VFM, it must be possible to objectively measure the performance of the service on an appropriate timescale. This is essential to ensure that the project objectives are achieved.

---

[30]   World Bank. 2020. *Benchmarking Infrastructure Development 2020: Assessing Regulatory Quality to Prepare, Procure, and Manage PPPs and Traditional Public Investment in Infrastructure Projects (English)*. Washington, DC. The countries analyzed are Cambodia, Indonesia, the Lao People's Democratic Republic, Malaysia, Mongolia, Myanmar, Papua New Guinea, the People's Republic of China, the Philippines, Samoa, Solomon Islands, Thailand, Timor-Leste, Tonga, Viet Nam, and Vanuatu.

[31]   World Bank. 2017. Public–Private Partnerships: Reference Guide, Version 3.0. Washington, DC. See Section 1.25 for a discussion of PPPs in fragile and conflict-affected states.

A Power Purchase Agreement (PPA) for supply of power, for example, has a wide range of objective performance standards such as output, availability, planned and unplanned outage duration, and annual generation that can be specified in the contract and continuously monitored and measured. Failure to meet the standards can result in penalties being imposed up to and including termination if the failure is major and prolonged. In contrast, a PPP for the provision of education services (a school) or health (a hospital) has a wide range of different performance measures; some are short term, some long term, some quantitative, and some qualitative.[32]

Infrastructure projects are complex, requiring upstream planning, project prioritization, sound frameworks for procurement of PPP projects, institutional capacities for public financial management and governance, and a sound business and policy environment. Given the complexity of infrastructure service contracts, the lack of monitoring and regulatory capacity in many can be problematic. Institutional weakness in concession contract monitoring can potentially undermine VFM during service delivery, as well as fiscal and debt sustainability. But all too often, this crucial requirement and the likely problems that can unfold are not considered during the key decision moments. There are PPP tool kits available that can help governments improve decision-making and determine if a PPP would be the best suited procurement option.[33]

Incentives and Risks
The key to a PPP offering VFM is efficient risk allocation, and the powers and incentives to mitigate and manage risk. The incentives need to be robust

and aligned with the quality of the service to be delivered. For example, if the government accepts land acquisition risk for a project, the private sector will logically seek compensation and penalties to be "kept whole" if the acquisition is not completed in the time allocated in the contract. These penalties incentivize the government to perform. Conversely, if the private sector is allocated the risks of construction, maintenance, and operating cost overruns through a fixed "availability payment" contract, they have the appropriate incentives to manage and mitigate the risks or face the financial consequences.[34]

Assessing Value for Money during Project Tendering
The tendering stage increasingly involves the application of quantitative VFM. The PSC estimates the fiscal costs if the government carries out the project through traditional public procurement. The data generated by the quantitative PSC are assessed against the cost of the PPP based on the bids received during the tendering process. This helps to confirm that the allocation of risk to the private sector under a PPP will deliver better VFM than the public option. As noted earlier, the PSC focuses mainly on risk-adjusted fiscal costs. VFM, on the other hand, is an analysis of a combination of costs and benefits to achieve the objectives of the project.

While in this tendering stage, there is likely to be enough information available to estimate a preliminary PSC, and the qualitative VFM analysis undertaken at the project-selection stage should be revised and updated. The combination of qualitative and quantitative analyses and data maximizes the information available to make decisions on the likely achievement of VFM.

---

[32] Global Infrastructure Hub. 2019. *Output Specifications for Quality Infrastructure.* Practical guidance with a focus on PPPs and other long-term contracts. This paper includes three social sector three case studies: Milton Hospital in Canada, Mersin Integrated Health Campus in Turkey, and Lewisham Grouped Schools in the United Kingdom. The paper identifies key issues for output specifications, performance measures, and reporting and contractual mechanisms for quality infrastructure.

[33] One such tool kit is The *PPP Toolkit for Improving PPP Decision Making Processes* (2010) published by the Ministry of Finance in India. It contains a set of decision-making tools to help PPP practitioners make decisions at each step of the PPP process. It provides templates for state highways, water and sanitation, ports, solid waste management, and urban transport. See Public Private Partnership in India | Toolkit for Decision Making Processes (pppinindia.gov.in). The World Bank has developed the Country PPP Readiness tool to assess a country's readiness to implement PPPs by reviewing the institutional and regulatory environment and comparing it to best practices. See Public-Private Partnerships (PPPs) - Tools (worldbank.org) for a full list of PPP tools.

[34] Global Infrastructure Hub. 2019. PPP Risk Allocation Tool. This web-based tool is designed to provide practical guidance and examples of risk allocation between the public and private sectors. It covers water and waste, transport, energy, communications, industrial parks, and social infrastructure for schools, hospitals, social housing, prisons, and government offices. See https://ppp-risk.gihub.org/.

Producing the Public Sector Comparator

The first step in the VFM calculation is to produce a raw PSC.[35] This estimates the whole-life baseline costs of the project if the government were to implement the project through a traditional procurement modality. It also accounts for any revenues that the government would receive by charging user fees. The PSC is a benchmark against which the government measures the fiscal costs of a project relative to alternative options for financing, funding, and delivering a project. It does not determine whether a project is affordable; the PSC provides a relative rather than an absolute measure. The raw PSC is a calculation of the net fiscal impact of the project. It includes a "competitive neutrality" analysis to adjust for any advantages or disadvantages that the government may have in implementing a public sector project, but that are not normally considered as project costs or benefits (such as tax liabilities). It also includes risk adjustment to take account of risks that are transferred to the private sector under a PPP. The costs of managing and bearing these risks would accrue to the government under traditional public procurement.

There are several approaches to valuing risks. Box 3 illustrates a simple probability-based approach to estimating and valuing the risk of construction cost overruns. More complex statistical methodologies such as Monte Carlo Simulations[36] are often used to assess costs associated with project risks. A typical example of statistical analysis is the probabilistic assessment of the risk of a project delay that results in additional costs and delays delivery of services from the project, resulting in additional and unanticipated project costs. Under the PPP alternative, delays and cost overruns in construction may be less probable. Based on a statistical analysis of the probability of delays and cost overruns associated with past similar projects in that geographic area, an assessment is made of the economic consequences and added financial cost of probable delays; this is added back into the PSC.

Conversion of the Raw Public Sector Comparator to an Adjusted Public Sector Comparator

The next step following calculation of the PSC is to create an adjusted PSC. The adjusted PSC normally involves converting project costs, so that these costs account for the risks that the government retains in traditional government procurement; in a PPP, these would be allocated to the private partner. These costs are derived from a review of the technical, economic, social, and governance (ESG), and climate analyses, and other studies that are part of the project appraisal process. The justification for the risk adjustment is that the costs associated with traditional public sector procurement and the PPP alternative need to show, as much as feasible, the same risk profiles. For example, if normally the construction risk is transferred to the private partner under a PPP, the PSC should replicate the costs that are attributable to carrying the construction risk. The economic and financial costs of estimated construction delays and cost overruns will be added back to determine the adjusted PSC.

Some countries make additional adjustments to the PSC to offset the cost advantages of a purely public option by making a "competitive neutrality" adjustment. The most common approach to competitive neutrality is to add back into the public option the effect of taxes on the private provider. This will duplicate the same taxes paid by the private provider and add them back into the public sector option to neutralize the effect of taxes on the public budget. Another adjustment is to include the cost that the government incurs for project management and transaction implementation, such as the cost of an independent expert to certify completion of construction milestones.

---

[35] Full details of how to construct PSC and undertake VFM analysis can be found in ADB's PPP operational plan. See ADB. *Public–Private Partnership Operational Plan 2012–2020.* Appendix 3.

[36] The Monte Carlo Simulation is a statistical method to model the probability of different outcomes using many randomly selected "what if" scenarios for each calculation. It provides a full range of possible outcomes and the probability of each outcome.

Box 3: Valuing Risks: A Probability-Based Approach

A PPP unit estimates that an infrastructure project will have construction costs of $80 million. This is the amount that the finance ministry would include in the budget—it is the raw PSC. Evidence from similar public procurement projects suggests that there is only a 10% probability that actual construction costs (including both cost and time overrun) will be the same as the base amount included in the raw PSC; most likely, it will exceed the initial base amount by around 20%. The project team also estimates that there is a further risk of a 25% increase and a smaller risk that costs will increase by up to 40%. In addition, there is a further possibility that costs may be 5% below the base amount.

Taking these probabilities into account, the likely costs can be plotted as a simple probability distribution.

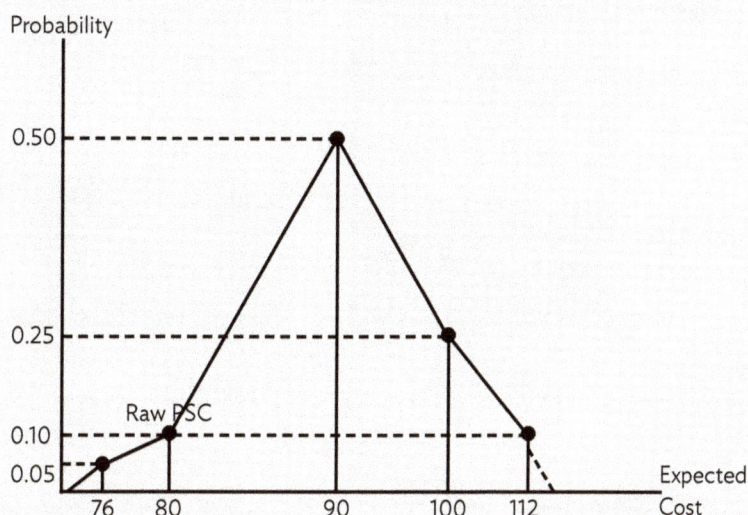

This analysis suggests that the most likely outcome is that construction costs will be $96 million and thus the value of this risk if transferred to the private sector would be $16 million. The project team will increase the raw PSC by $16 million to take account of the risk that the public sector would transfer to the private sector in a PPP. This example illustrates the assumptions and need for data inherent in the estimation of a quantitative PSC. In real world cases, and especially in developing countries, it is highly unlikely that a government would have a database of comparable projects with initial cost estimates and cost overruns to enable an accurate estimate of the probabilities used in this example.

PPP = public–private partnership, PSC = public sector comparator.

Source: Authors (Shur and Bloomgarden).

Comparing Two Procurement Routes: Public–Private Partnership and Public

After calculating the adjusted PSC, the next step is to compare the net present value (NPV) of each alternative—the PPP and traditional public investment—and determine a discount rate to apply to the cost projections. The application of the discount rate in VFM analysis varies around the world. Options for calculating the discount rate may include the opportunity cost of government funds based on the government risk-free borrowing rate, or the degree of risk for each individual project. Since the discount rate greatly influences the results of the VFM calculation, it is important to carefully choose and justify which method to use.

VFM is calculated as the NPV of the cost of the public sector option **plus** any adjustment for additional regulatory costs **minus** the NPV of the PPP option based on construction costs, operations and maintenance, renewal and replacement costs, and adjustments for probable cost overruns and competitive neutrality. Once the government contracting authority

Figure 4:   Example of Value for Money Comparison

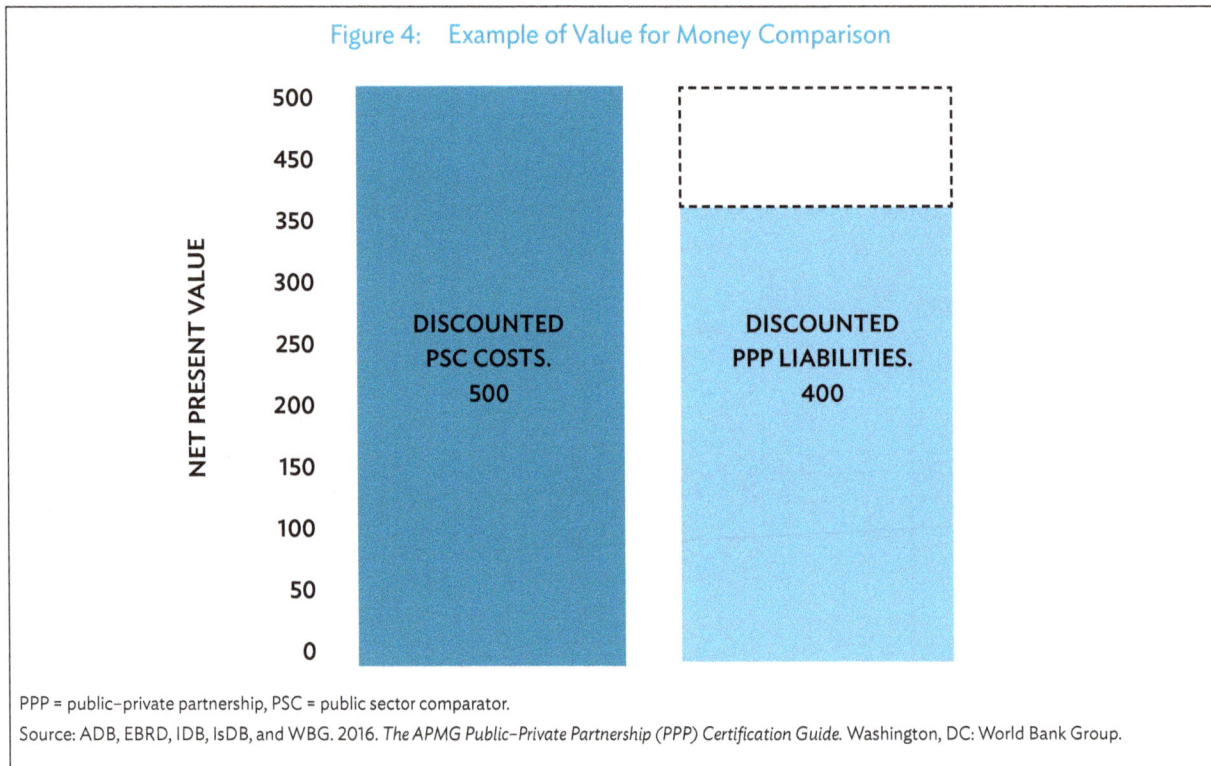

PPP = public–private partnership, PSC = public sector comparator.

Source: ADB, EBRD, IDB, IsDB, and WBG. 2016. *The APMG Public–Private Partnership (PPP) Certification Guide.* Washington, DC: World Bank Group.

has reduced the PSC and PPP alternatives to one NPV number, the final step determines which procurement modality is the best choice to implement the project. The PPP offers better VFM when the NPV costs of the PPP are lower than the NPV costs of the PSC (Figure 4).

Limitations of the Public Sector Comparator Methodology

The use of the PSC methodology has been called into question due to concerns about the quality of data and ability to manipulate results. A House of Lords review of the PSC in the United Kingdom (UK) found that the absence of useful data and methodological concerns have, in practice, served to limit its usefulness. Although the PSC has limitations for determining VFM, the government responded to the study saying VFM can be useful for decision-making when used in combination with qualitative VFM analysis.[37] *The World Bank Research Observer* similarly reported widespread global criticism

of PSC analysis due to concerns about the accuracy of data and the potential for project teams to manipulate the results.[38]

The treatment of revenue is another contentious issue. Some countries (such as France) assume that PPPs are better at generating revenues than a public sector entity. Other countries (such as the Republic of Korea) assume that revenues would be the same in a PPP and or a traditional public investment project. These countries typically restrict the ability of public sector agencies to undertake noncore commercial activities; therefore, ancillary revenues generated by a project are assumed to happen only in PPPs.[39] The lack of a standardized approach underlines the need for caution in relying on a PSC number rather than focusing on which type of arrangement will best achieve the project objectives.

---

[37]   United Kingdom National Audit Office. 2013. *Review of the VFM assessment process for PFI.* Briefing for the House of Commons Treasury Select Committee.

[38]   Leigland, J. 2018. Public–Private Partnerships in Developing Countries: The Emerging Evidence-Based Critique. *The World Bank Research Observer.* Volume 33, Issue 1.

[39]   See the People's Republic of China TA 8940: Municipality-Level Public–Private Partnership (PPP) Operational Framework for Chongqing.

Box 4: Southeast Asia: Experience with Quantitative Public Sector Comparator

Absolute value for money refers to VFM for traditional public procurement or a PPP, but without a comparison to determine which option is more efficient. Relative VFM compares the value for money of a PPP to the value for money if the government were to deliver the project as a traditional public sector project.

A 2018 OECD survey found that half of Southeast Asian economies implement relative VFM using public sector comparators to assess if a PPP project is a more efficient option than a traditionally procured infrastructure project. The survey also showed the following in relation to Southeast Asia:

(i)   Seventy percent of countries undertake absolute VFM for all traditional infrastructure procurement and PPPs. Myanmar and Singapore assess relative VFM only for projects that exceed a particular threshold.

(ii)   All ten surveyed countries use PPPs, but institutional arrangements vary.

(iii)   Seven out of the ten countries have PPP units. However, only four have created PPP units within the finance ministry, which can help ensure fiscal assessments of PPPs.

(iv)   Most countries find it hard to judge if a PPP performs better than traditional infrastructure procurement. Countries reported that lack of data or expertise makes it challenging to determine the performance of PPPs compared to traditional public investments.

Notes:

Data are from the 2018 OECD Budget Practices and Procedures Survey for Asian Countries. Survey responses came mainly from senior budget officials and are self-assessments of processes and procedures for VFM at the federal government level.

The ten countries surveyed were Brunei Darussalam, Cambodia, Indonesia, the Lao PDR, Malaysia, Myanmar, the Philippines, Singapore, Thailand, and Viet Nam.

A PPP unit is an organizational unit set up to promote and improve the quality of PPPs across government departments. Its functions vary but can include promotion, planning, design, and procurement of PPPs.

ADB = Asian Development Bank, OECD = Organization for Economic Co-operation and Development, PPP = public–private partnership, VFM = value for money.

Source: ADB and OECD. 2019. Government at a Glance Southeast Asia 2019.

Other Quantitative Value for Money Analysis Methods

Due to limited data and ability to value risk, some countries use other methods either as a substitute for or in addition to the PSC. These alternatives include reference class forecasting and shadow bid models.

Reference class forecasting. Reference class forecasting (RCF) is a method of forecasting future outcomes by analyzing comparable past projects and their outcomes. It is used to eliminate optimism bias in demand forecasts for infrastructure assets. The first example of RCF implementation is described in Flyvbjerg (2006).[40] In 2004, the Government of the UK used RCF for the projected capital costs of a project to extend Edinburgh Trams. The original forecast estimated a cost of £255 million. Based on a reference class of comparable rail projects, the reference class forecast estimated a cost of £320 million. Since the Edinburgh forecast, RCF has been applied to other projects in the UK, including the £15 billion ($29 billion) Crossrail Project in London. After 2004, the Netherlands, Denmark, and Switzerland also implemented RCF. A study conducted for Hong Kong, China's Development Bureau compared the forecast costs and duration of investment projects with actual outcomes based on a sample of 863 projects. This study identified optimism bias in overestimating demand and underestimating costs in the initial estimates and contributed to improved future forecasting models.[41] In the Republic of Ireland,

---

40   Flyvbjerg, B. 2006. From Nobel Prize to Project Management: Getting Risks Right. *Project Management Journal.* 37 (3). pp. 5–15.
41   B. Flyvberg, C. Hon, and W.H. Fok. 2016. *Reference Class Forecasting for Hong Kong's Major Roadworks Projects.* ICE Proceedings, Hong Kong, China.

Transport Infrastructure Ireland (TII) changed its cost forecasting process through preparation of guidance on the use of RCF.[42] TII's reference classes will be updated on a regular basis to incorporate data from new projects to ensure data continue to be relevant. It will also provide data to enhance the effectiveness of risk management and help to capture lessons learned from prior projects.

Shadow bid models. Several jurisdictions such as the UK, Australia, and New Zealand require that in addition to preparing the PSC, implementing agencies must also develop a shadow bid model (SBM) to compare SBM and PSC outcomes. The SBM estimates a private bid price, considering the private capital structure and payment terms. Inputs (including the discount rate) should be verified and stress tested with input from the ministries of finance. These models should be updated as new data become available during the procurement process. For economic infrastructure projects, if there is a government equity investment, the PSC principles should also include a commercial rate of return on the government's equity. Bidders should also be advised if there are differences between the SBM assumptions and the bidders' assumptions, especially in regard to calculation methods. This is to avoid overpriced bids arising from different assumptions in the SBM and PSC models.

Qualitative Analysis of Project Objectives

Despite the importance of examining project objectives and benefits as part of a VFM analysis, relatively few governments do this based on a purely quantitative approach. As mentioned, New Zealand's approach provides a step in the right direction by including a simple, quantitative cost–benefit comparison of PPP and public procurement.

The Castalia (2016) guidance for Chongqing recommends that, in response to the limitations

associated with a cost-focused VFM analysis, a principles-based framework is required.[43] This framework focuses on understanding whether the private sector has the incentives to deliver the project's objectives better than the public sector. It asks four broad questions:

(i)   Can the private sector deliver the project objectives at lower cost?

(ii) What are the key risks to delivering project objectives?

(iii) Are key risks effectively transferred to the private sector?

(iv) Is the private sector incentivized and capable of managing transferred risks?

Securing Value for Money during Project Implementation

Contract management is often neglected area in PPP analysis and discussions, which tend to focus more on the project preparation stage of the project cycle. However, contract management is the "Achilles' heel" of any PPP governance framework in DMCs precisely because (i) it gets much less attention and support, and (ii) it is so crucial for the ultimate VFM outcome of PPPs. Even a well-designed project can fail to deliver on its objectives if not properly managed during implementation and can result in higher costs and lower-quality service. The complexity, risks, and long-term nature of infrastructure requires that VFM be guarded throughout the life cycle of a project. After a project is approved and under implementation, a reassessment of VFM can provide valuable lessons for future projects.

Effective contract management is related to the quality of project preparation. Poorly prepared projects can result in delays and cost overruns that undermine the achievement of VFM during the implementation phase. Project preparation activities that affect performance during construction and service delivery include, but are

---

[42]   Transport Infrastructure Ireland. 2019. *Reference Class Forecasting Guidelines for use in connection with National Roads Projects.* This document presents reference class forecasting as a method for explicitly trying to eliminate the optimism bias in project budgets and schedules. It compares the project to 20–30 similar projects. It identifies the risk variables, such as project delays or cost overruns and the probability distribution of these risks across the project sample, and adjusts the estimate of risk by determining whether the proposed project is more or less risky than the sample of projects.

[43]   ADB, Castalia Consultant report to the ADB. 2016. *Municipality-Level Public-Private Partnership (PPP) Operational Framework for Chongqing – PPP Value for Money Guidance Note.*

Figure 5:   Steps for Developing and Implementing the Government's Contract Management Strategy

Ongoing information collection and analysis

| Procurement phase | → | Input contract management expertise into RFP requirements
Start developing contract management strategy |

| Contract execution and financial close | ⇢ | Within 60 days of financial close have approval of contract management plan and publish contract |

| Construction phase | → | Develop and finalize contract administration manual (or similar tools)

Transition project director to contract director |

| Service delivery phase | → | Implementation and ongoing review of contract management framework |

RFP = request for proposal.

Source: Partnerships Victoria. 2018. Contract Management Guide. Department of Treasury and Finance, Australia. Available at: https://www.dtf.vic.gov.au/public-private-partnerships/policy-guidelines-and-templates

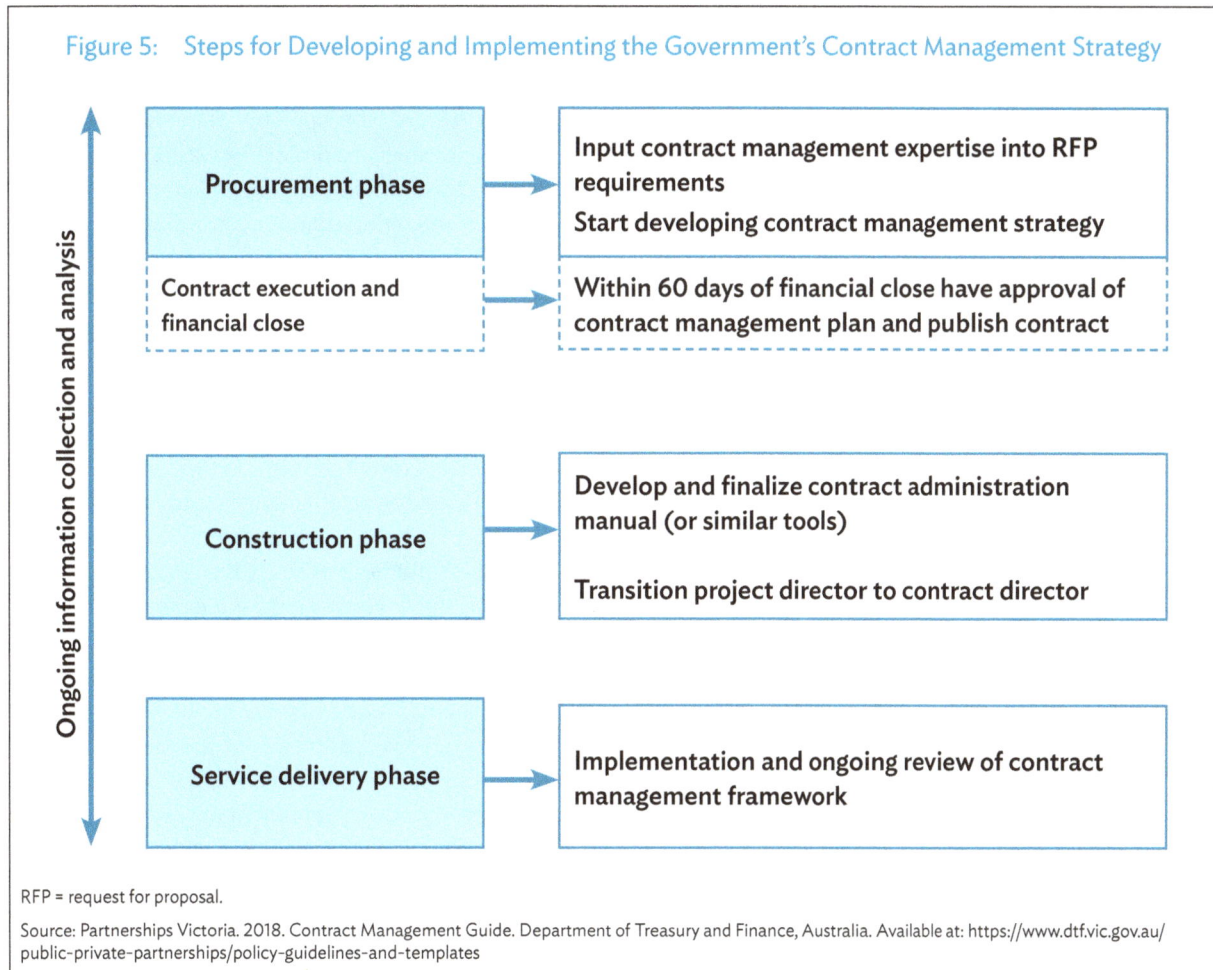

not limited to, acquiring land rights, securing sustainable financing such as viability gap financing, obtaining concessional MDB loans or in-kind government support, and establishing a project unit that can effectively manage the PPP contract. As noted earlier, weak project preparation and contract management capacity can contribute to renegotiations that often result in reduced VFM.[44]

The government should develop a project management strategy starting with the procurement phase of project preparation. The strategy should lay out the contractual obligations of the public and private parties to the proposed contract. These obligations will form part of the government's request for proposals and will be included in a contract administration manual for the construction and service delivery phase of the project. This is exemplified the 2018 *Contract Management Guide* of Partnerships Victoria (Figure 5).

Securing Value for Money Following Contract Completion

The ability of a project to achieve the intended VFM can change over the life cycle of a project. Change orders, renegotiations, and the macro environment can alter the ability of a project over time to achieve its objectives. For this reason, an ex-post analysis of VFM can help a government learn from experience

---

[44]   Bloomgarden, D. 2020. Case Study 5: Managing Public–Private Partnerships Renegotiation *Enhancing Government Effectiveness and Transparency: The Fight Against Corruption.* World Bank. This case study demonstrates the importance of fiscal transparency, project preparation, independent expert advice, and proactive contract management to avoid costly contract renegotiation.

and make adjustments to increase accountability for outcomes. In addition, an ex-post VFM assessment can result in lessons learned for the development of future PPP projects. Ex-post audits are not a common feature in emerging PPP markets in developing Asia. Australia and the UK are examples of mature PPP markets that carry out ex-post audits of PPP projects to evaluate the potential for achieving VFM identified in the project preparation stage.

Case Studies: Indonesia, Philippines, Viet Nam, Republic of Korea, and Armenia

Indonesia

The Government of Indonesia established the Indonesia Infrastructure Guarantee Fund (IIGF) in 2009 as an independent state-owned enterprise (SOE) to be the sole institution or the "single window"—for appraising, structuring, and providing government guarantees for PPP. To further support the implementation of PPPs, the government established in 2015 a PPP Unit located in the Ministry of Finance. This unit, which received support under ADB policy-based loans,[45] is responsible for identifying, screening, and preparing PPP projects. It is also responsible for project approval and oversight of the national PPP program. It reviews the pipeline of priority PPP projects based on VFM to propose a shortlist of bankable projects for preparation.

Overall, the Government of Indonesia has a relatively strong PPP framework for carrying out VFM. According to the World Bank's 2020 report *Benchmarking Infrastructure Development*, Indonesia's overall quality

of project preparation procedures and regulations scores higher than the global average for all developing countries, with a score of 51 out of 100.[46] Not every PPP project requires the approval of the Ministry of Finance. However, if a project has a government guarantee then it requires approval from the Ministry of Finance or the Indonesian Infrastructure Guarantee Fund before bidding. The same applies for projects that request support from such facilities as the Project Development Facility (PDF) or the Viability Gap Fund (VGF). The government includes PPP direct liabilities in the national budget. Contingent liabilities arising from government guarantees for PPP projects are managed and monitored within the Ministry of Finance (Directorate of Financing Strategy and Portfolio). Such liabilities are also reported annually as part of the Statement of Fiscal Risks submitted and presented by the government to Parliament in the Budget Note.

The government is required to carry out risk identification and mitigation as well as risk allocation. IMF's PIMA assessment showed there is no standard methodology for risk assessment. However, the government has an action plan that addresses the issues raised in the PIMA assessment.[47] In addition, Indonesia's public sector is highly decentralized, with multiple levels of government agencies. This makes it difficult to ensure whole-of-government coordination among stakeholders and to define the responsibility of each agency during project preparation. It further subjects the process to project delays. Some government agencies also lack adequate capacity to plan, prepare and procure projects that consistently meet best global practices.[48] The government is addressing this issue by providing support to government contracting agencies through the PPP unit and the inter-agency Committee on Acceleration of Priority Infrastructure, which hires qualified advisors for project preparation. The committee is the one-stop contact for all government agencies and

45   ADB. 2020. Thematic Evaluation of ADB Support for PPPs 2009–2018. Annex: Country Case Assessment: Indonesia. ADB provides assistance through a multitranche loan between 2014 and 2016 to strengthen PPP policies and establish and operationalize the PPP Office. It is called the Stepping Up Investments for Growth Acceleration Program. It has three subprograms (SPs) implemented from 2013 to 2018. SP1 was approved in 2014, SP2 in 2016, and SP3 in 2018. The PPP Unit was established in SP2.

46   World Bank. 2020. *Benchmarking Infrastructure Development*. Washington, DC.

47   *Indonesia Public Investment Management Assessment: Experiences from Indonesia*. 2019. Presentation by the Ministry of National Development Planning/National Development Planning Agency at the Tokyo Fiscal Forum 2019.

48   ADB. 2019. *Public–Private Partnership Monitor*. Manila.

investors interested in infrastructure projects that are classified as high priority for the country.

Philippines

The Philippines has several of the key ingredients for successful PPP implementation. According to the World Bank's *Benchmarking Infrastructure Development* report, the Philippines scores a high 79 out of 100 when it comes to the quality of project preparation, which includes implementation of VFM assessments. This compares to an average score of 40 for all developing countries in the same income group and a regional average of 35. The Philippines also scores higher than its income group and regional comparators in terms of procurement regulations and policies.[49] Overall, the Philippines has a strong institutional framework for national and sectoral planning, budgeting for investment (including contingent liabilities), and availability of funding. This framework contributes to VFM analysis. All PPP contracts contain clauses on dispute resolution that, depending on the contract, is to be undertaken either internationally or in the Philippines.

The country has a long-term vision and medium-term development plan, the 5-year Philippine Development Plan (PDP). The PDP, in turn, is linked to regional and local plans. The PDP provides a comprehensive framework for the medium-term Public Investment Program (PIP) and the Comprehensive and Integrated Infrastructure Program (CIIP). The Philippines' comprehensive planning process is overseen by the National Economic and Development Authority (NEDA), an independent cabinet-level agency of the government, headed by the President as chair of the NEDA board. NEDA is also responsible for the evaluation, review, and monitoring of infrastructure projects under the CIIP, in line with the government's priority of increasing investment spending for the growing demand for quality infrastructure facilities. NEDA manages the PIP with recommendations from line agencies, but it is the Investment Coordination Committee (ICC) which approves all national

investment projects above a threshold and all PDP-funded projects. The ICC Secretariat is in NEDA. The ICC has three steps of endorsements or approvals. Line agencies submit proposals to the ICC Secretariat, which reviews the proposal and produces an evaluation report, including an assessment of the project's economic rate of return. The report is submitted to the ICC-Technical Board (ICC-TB) which includes representatives from oversight agencies. If the project passes, the ICC-TB endorses it to the ICC Cabinet Committee for first level approval. If approved, it is then submitted to the NEDA Board for final approval. PPP projects also require ICC approval. Recent changes mean that the ICC will decide whether a project will be a PPP, a hybrid, or public project.

The PPP Center serves as the central agency for all PPP projects in the Philippines. It supports implementing agencies in project preparation, manages the Project Development and Monitoring Facility, provides project advisory and facilitation services, and offers capacity building support. The PPP Center support helps to empower government-owned-and controlled corporations, national government agencies, government financial institutions, local government units, as well as state universities and colleges, and the private sector to help develop and implement infrastructure projects.

A critical component of VFM is ensuring that all risks relevant to the project have been identified, allocated, and mitigated. The risk assessment is carried out by the Department of Finance. The government uses a generic preferred risk allocation matrix (GPRAM) that lists the risk allocation preferences and risk mitigation measures for the development and implementation of PPP projects. The GPRAM includes guidance for regulatory risks (e.g., guaranteeing tariff adjustments by formula), compensation for competing facilities, and payments arising from termination (such as government or concessionaire default, or force majeure).[50] Although the government is open to unsolicited proposals to accelerate its infrastructure plan, the amended build–operate–transfer (BOT) law and implementing regulations require that these proposals contain a new

---

[49] World Bank. 2020. *Benchmarking Infrastructure Development.* Washington, DC.

[50] ADB. 2017. Scaling Up Infrastructure Investment in the Philippines: Role of Public Private Partnerships and Issues. *Southeast Asia Working Paper Series.* No. 13. Manila.

concept or technology and require no government equity, subsidy, or guarantee. The government then invites competitive proposals from other companies.[51]

To mitigate potential fiscal affordability risks to VFM, ADB implemented a policy-based loan (completed in 2019) and a separate technical assistance grant to support the government's ability to ensure that funding is available and that contingent liabilities arising from PPP contracts can be tracked. A contingent liabilities fund was established to meet the government's contractual obligations in PPPs. To ensure the continued fiscal sustainability of the PPP portfolio, the government established an inter-agency working group to monitor contingent liabilities. According to an evaluation of ADB support for PPPs during 2009–2019, ADB has been actively engaged in providing loans for PPP projects and technical assistance to help create fiscal space, assist with budget planning, and support management for both national government and local governments. ADB has also provided support to the PPP Center and implementing agencies to develop and manage PPP projects.[52]

Viet Nam

In Viet Nam, VFM in PPPs has been closely linked to the evolution of the legislative framework for PPPs. In June 2020, the National Assembly of Viet Nam approved the PPP Law, which established an overall legal framework for PPP projects with the goal of attracting more private investment in Viet Nam's infrastructure. The law became effective on 1 January 2021 and replaces the earlier PPP regulations under Decree No. 63/2018/ND-CP dated 4 May 2018 (Decree 63).

The new law will contribute to VFM in PPP procurement. Until the passing of the new law, the private sector had to understand a complicated framework of legislative instruments and legal provisions applicable to their infrastructure project.

This complexity has not acted as a complete deterrent; Viet Nam has signed 140 projects under BOT contracts and another eight projects under other types of PPP contracts since the initial amendment to the Law on Foreign Investment to accommodate BOT schemes and other PPP projects in 1992.[53] More than $24 billion has been invested in the country's PPPs.

According to the World Bank's *Benchmarking Infrastructure Development* report, Viet Nam scores a relatively high 70 out of 100 in the quality of project preparation, which includes implementation of VFM assessments. This compares to an average score of 40 for all developing countries in the same income group and a regional average of 35. Viet Nam also scores higher than its income group and higher than the global average for developing countries for the quality of its procurement regulations and policies.[54] The government includes PPP costs in the national budget, including the cost of liabilities arising from PPPs based on information available before launching the procurement. The regulatory framework includes PPPs in the medium-term budgetary framework and the national public investment system. It provides procedures to ensure PPPs are in accordance with other public investment priorities. However, the government does not disclose PPP liabilities (explicit and implicit, direct, and contingent) that is available to the public through an online platform.

Overall, the new PPP law provides a more transparent and unified legal framework to guide decision-making for the efficient allocation of risks. As noted in a recent ADB article, the law is a "crucial milestone," but now is the time for implementation.[55] Implementation of the law requires a high standard of project preparation. The ADB blog argues that project preparation goes beyond financial structuring to allocate risks to parties that can best manage the risk. It also requires application of the G20 Principles for QII that emphasize life-cycle costs, environmental and social costs and benefits, disaster resilience, and governance. The blog also makes the point that guarantees could play a greater role in mobilizing private investment to

---

[51]   ADB. 2020. *PPP Monitor Philippines.*

[52]   ADB. 2020. *ADB Support for Public–Private Partnerships, 2009–2019: Thematic Evaluation.* Independent Evaluation Department, ADB. Manila.

[53]   Government's Report No. 25/BC-CP on the status of implementation of PPP projects in Viet Nam (2019), Viet Nam.

[54]   World Bank. 2020. *Benchmarking Infrastructure Development.* Washington, DC.

[55]   Lambert, D. 2021. Viet Nam's Public–Private Partnerships Law is Up and Running. What's next? *Asian Development Bank Blog.* Manila, Philippines.

meet Viet Nam's need for infrastructure finance. In the medium term, the government will need to ensure that it is able to fund preparation costs and consider a mechanism to recover these costs and recycle the funds in the preparation of new projects.

Republic of Korea

The Republic of Korea experienced a serious shortage of infrastructure facilities in the 1990s. In response, the government began to push for PPP projects in earnest with the August 1994 enactment of the Act on Promotion of Private Capital Investment in Social Overhead Capital. Toward the end of the decade, the government developed the legislative framework through the Act on Private Participation in Infrastructure, enacted in December 1998, which among other things, sought to boost PPPs by introducing a minimum revenue guarantee (MRG).[56]

It soon became apparent that the MRG did not present VFM to the government. By the end of 2008, 36 out of 145 signed contracts included MRG clauses.

Criticisms against MRG included that the government took most of the risks, but still provided high returns to the private PPP party, and that the scheme provided private investors with incentives to overestimate future demand. In October 2009, the MRG was abolished and replaced by a new risk-sharing scheme. Table 3 outlines the key differences.

Importantly, the revised scheme promotes VFM in that while the government shares investment risk, it does so only within the limit of the government's cost of the project if it were to be procured as a public project. In other words, the cost arising from the PSC, determined prior to contract signing through a VFM test, is a ceiling on the government's exposure.

The Republic of Korea's approach to VFM appears on first assessment to mirror that of Australia's where PPPs must pass an investment decision, as outlined in Figure 6. In making the investment decision, the Ministry of Strategy and Finance (MOSF) reviews and establishes the annual aggregate investment ceiling subsequent to the procuring ministry's request for the investment ceiling. However, it is worth noting that

Table 3: Risk-Sharing Scheme versus Minimum Revenue Guarantee

	New Risk-Sharing Scheme	MRG
Government	Supports the private sector's investment recovery by setting the PSC as a ceiling	Guarantees certain level of revenue
Private Sector	Low-Risk, Low-Return - Project IRR is comparable to government bond yield (interest payment not included) - Government subsidies withdrawn	Low-Risk, High-Return - 65%-90% of the projected revenue guaranteed - Government subsidies not withdrawn
Coverage Period	The overall period of operation * long-term support at low IRR	A portion of the total operation period (e.g. 10 years) * Short-term support at high IRR
Impact	Investment risk borne by the private sector is mitigated with greater motivation for profit	Pro: Encourages private sector participation in PPPs Con: May result in the private sector's moral hazard

IRR = internal rate of return, MRG = minimum revenue guarantee, PPP = public–private partnership, PSC = public sector comparator.
Sources: Public–Private Partnership Infrastructure Projects: Case Studies from the Republic of Korea, Presentation to UNESCAP; Hyeon, P. 2012. Government Support for PPP Projects in Korea. Presentation at United Nations Economic and Social Commission for Asia and the Pacific (UNESCAP). Thailand.

[56] Jay-Hyung, K. et al. 2011. *Public–Private Partnership Infrastructure Projects: Case Studies from the Republic of Korea Volume 1: Institutional Arrangements and Performance.* Asian Development Bank. Philippines.

Figure 6:   Value for Money in Build–Transfer–Lease Projects in the Republic of Korea

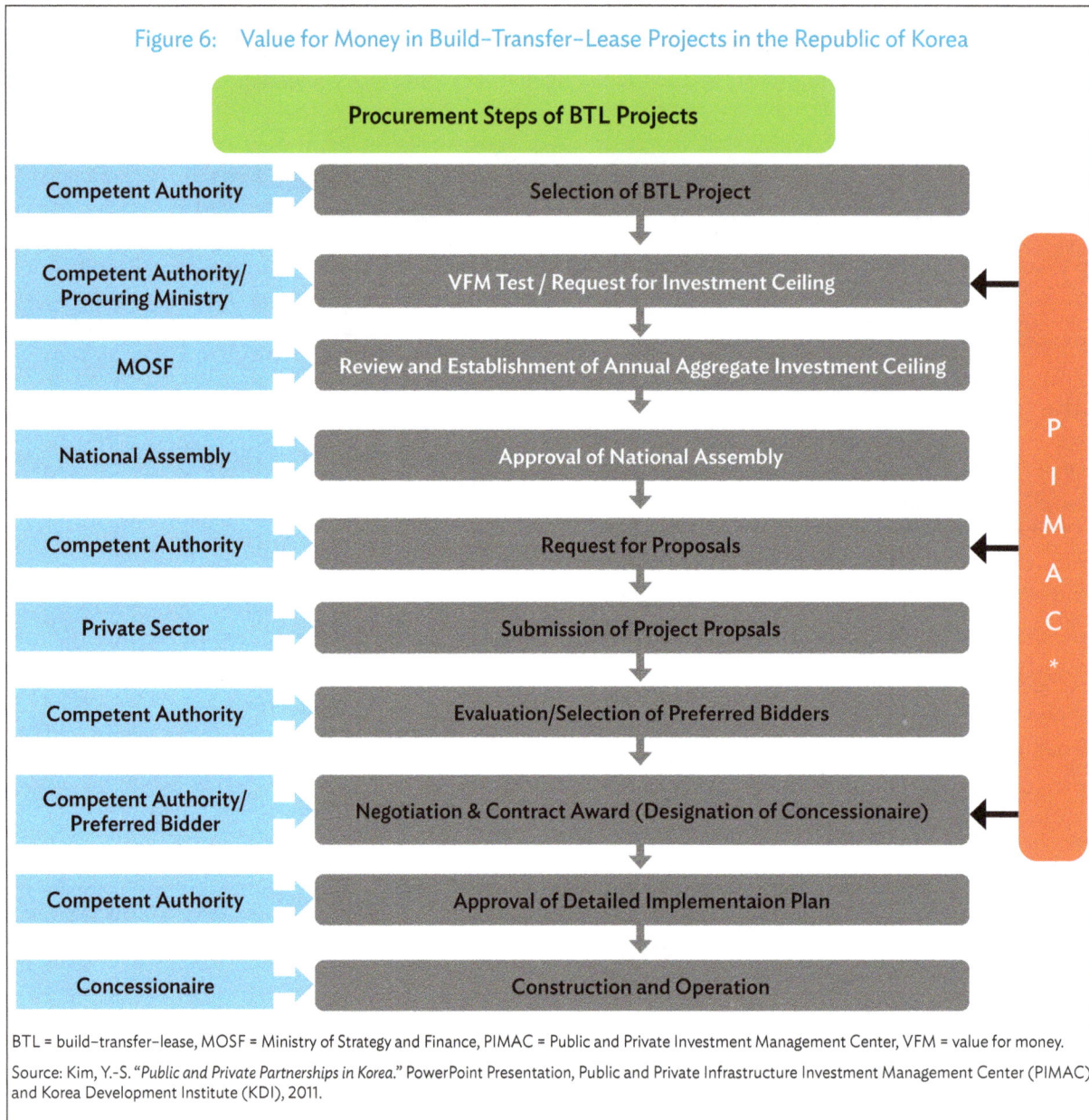

Procurement Steps of BTL Projects

Authority	Step
Competent Authority	Selection of BTL Project
Competent Authority/ Procuring Ministry	VFM Test / Request for Investment Ceiling
MOSF	Review and Establishment of Annual Aggregate Investment Ceiling
National Assembly	Approval of National Assembly
Competent Authority	Request for Proposals
Private Sector	Submission of Project Propsals
Competent Authority	Evaluation/Selection of Preferred Bidders
Competent Authority/ Preferred Bidder	Negotiation & Contract Award (Designation of Concessionaire)
Competent Authority	Approval of Detailed Implementaion Plan
Concessionaire	Construction and Operation

PIMAC*

BTL = build–transfer–lease, MOSF = Ministry of Strategy and Finance, PIMAC = Public and Private Investment Management Center, VFM = value for money.

Source: Kim, Y.-S. *"Public and Private Partnerships in Korea."* PowerPoint Presentation, Public and Private Infrastructure Investment Management Center (PIMAC) and Korea Development Institute (KDI), 2011.

this formal MOSF sign-off is limited to build–transfer–lease (BTL) PPPs. BTL is the default procurement method for availability payment-type PPPs as used for schools, dormitories, and military housing. This is because of the direct government payment associated with these schemes.

Interestingly, "economic" PPPs, such as road, seaport, and railway projects, which are typically procured as build–transfer–operate (BTO) PPPs, avoid this same level of MOSF scrutiny for fiscal cost and risk,

as shown in Figure 6. The role of MOSF is limited to the initial establishment of the annual aggregate investment ceiling, whereas there is an ongoing role for the Public and Private Infrastructure Management Center (PIMAC), a subsidiary of the government-run think tank, the Korea Development Institute (KDI). This differs from the approach of countries such as Australia, New Zealand, and South Africa, for example, where respective ministries of finance review projects for affordability, VFM, and fiscal risk post-negotiation and prior to awarding the contract to ensure that the risk allocation and fiscal limits resemble those of the business case approved for funding.

Armenia

The Government of Armenia has implemented several measures to strengthen public debt and fiscal risk management in support of fiscally responsible and planning-relevant PPP development.[57] ADB supported these efforts (including the strengthening of fiscal risk management) through programmatic assistance to Armenia (2017–2018) and stand-alone policy-based assistance (2019). Before these reforms, fiscal risk management was incomplete in scope. For example, it did not vet new infrastructure plans, lacked analytic methodologies, and did not include mitigation responsibilities or risk management. In addition, private provision of public infrastructure was not supported by an adequate legal or regulatory framework and was not done in a transparent manner without strong fiscal controls.

The government also took steps to strengthen its institutional capacity to enhance effective management of the risks that can affect fiscal stability. First, it approved the charter of a new Fiscal Risks and Statistics Department to elevate its institutional role the within Ministry of Finance from a division to a department. And second, it updated the Roadmap of Fiscal Risks Management Improvement to establish an integrated framework for risk management.

In June 2019, Armenia approved a new PPP law. This law excluded unsolicited proposals from its scope, provided greater clarity on the institutional responsibilities for PPP pipeline development and on the criteria for PPP development and approval, and made the Ministry of Finance a principal gatekeeper for PPP approvals. To promote stakeholder awareness and reform effectiveness, and based on the new law, the government distributed for inter-ministerial consultations a draft government decree as well as methodologies, regulations, and manuals to underpin the operational framework for PPPs.

To integrate PPPs with public investment management functions, the Ministry of Economy set up a PPP policy unit within the newly created Public Investment Policy Department. More recently, it approved a full-fledged Public Investment Management Framework Decree to govern all public investment decisions and procurement choices.

The institutionalization of an effective PPP operational and legal framework provides guidance to the government to develop PPP transactions that are relevant to Armenia's national investment priorities and fiscally responsible. Continuing ADB technical assistance focuses on strengthening institutional capacity to assess and manage risks in the stock of current concession projects.

During 2020–2021, the authorities steadily focused on progressing toward four key policy objectives. The first is to complete a full-fledged monitoring and risk-vetting framework for PPPs with fiscal affordability rules and linkage to Armenia's new fiscal rule. The fiscal risk management department at the Ministry of Finance prepared a more comprehensive Fiscal Risks Statement for the budget law for 2021. This has now been updated and upgraded further in the context of the Medium-Term Expenditure Framework update exercise completed in July 2021. A PPP Contingent Liabilities Decree, with requirements and methodologies for identifying risks and reporting in state budget documentation, as well as requirements for benchmarking against PPP fiscal affordability ceilings, was approved by the Cabinet of Ministers of Armenia on 6 November 2020.

---

[57]   Case study provided by Joao Pedro Farinha, principal financial sector economist, ADB.

4. Key Governance Conclusions for Supporting Value for Money Analysis in Developing Member Countries

Planning the Infrastructure Portfolio

VFM depends on the strength of the infrastructure governance framework. A sound governance framework recognizes that VFM is not a guaranteed outcome from PPP procurement. Rather, it must be secured not at a single point in time, but together with its intended socioeconomic and environmental benefits achieved over the entire project life cycle. Regardless of the rigor with which the various VFM techniques, guidance, and analyses are applied, they will not be successful and VFM will not be achieved if the country's overall governance framework for PPPs is flawed or nonexistent. Weaknesses in infrastructure governance lead to opaque decision-making and exacerbate fiscal risks. Simply put, VFM analysis cannot mask deficiencies in the overall PPP project governance framework; it is only when the latter is effectively designed and established that proper decision-making can be consistently expected and VFM become a likely outcome.[58]

Funding decisions should be made independent of whether a project is to be delivered as a PPP or a more traditional public option. The funding decision for a project should reflect that it is part of a strategic/sector priority plan for infrastructure and fits within a medium-term fiscal and budget framework regardless of how the project is delivered. Governments need to budget resources for the right projects. It is only after the funding decision that governments should consider how to invest and whether to deliver the project as PPP. For this, governments

need to implement VFM within a system of sound infrastructure governance—robust frameworks and institutions to plan, allocate, and implement PPP projects. It is critical to distinguish between investment decisions on the one hand and finance and delivery decisions on the other.

Selection of Projects

Fiscal space should not be used as a justification for selecting a PPP. The reason for choosing PPP over traditional public procurement is that it delivers better VFM through private sector risk management and efficiency. PPPs, even if funded wholly or in part by the private sector, do not provide extra fiscal capacity. The government remains responsible for direct or indirect contingent fiscal liabilities when it controls the services that the operator must provide with the PPP asset, sets the price, and bears the ultimate responsibility for the continuous delivery of the infrastructure service to the public.

Project Appraisal and Procurement

VFM tells us which method of procurement—traditional or PPP—is most likely to achieve project objectives. VFM analysis should focus on optimizing benefits and costs to achieve project objectives. It should assess whether the private sector is incentivized and able to efficiently manage and mitigate risks and deliver greater benefits than the public sector procurement option. Lastly, through

---

[58]   E. Engle, R. D. Fischer, and A. Galetovic. 2020. When and How to Use Public–Private Partnerships in Infrastructure: Lessons from the International Experience. Forthcoming in Glaeser and Poterba, eds. *Economic Analysis and Infrastructure Investment.*

qualitative analysis, it should protect authorities against low-balling and other strategic bidding phenomena that, through opaque renegotiation pressures, end up significantly changing the VFM equation and outcomes.

Project Implementation

VFM tests should be done both before procurement and after the project begins operations. VFM analysis is normally done at the project preparation stage and when comparisons can be made with the bids received. Ex-ante VFM cannot tell whether the project will fully realize the promised financial advantages of a PPP. Refinancing at lower costs during the operational phase can also affect VFM. For example, in a road project, if refinancing savings are shared with the government or used to lower toll rates, this can improve VFM. The quality of subcontractors responsible for maintenance will also impact revenue streams. If a road designed to carry 100 vehicles per minute only carries 60 vehicles per minute due to poor maintenance, this will significantly affect VFM by reducing revenue streams. VFM should also be done as an ex-post evaluation when the project commences operations to provide lessons for future PPP projects.

Appendixes

Appendix 1: Qualitative Checklist for Public–Private Partnership Value for Money

The following table provides a set of practical qualitative questions that can be used to assess whether the public–private partnership (PPP) procurement route is feasible. A "yes" answer to most of these questions would indicate that a PPP could deliver value for money; a "no" answer would indicate that the PPP route may not be desirable. The checklist should be part of an overall analysis of the social, economic, environmental, climate, and financial costs and benefits.

1	Does the project improve market supply or lead to better prices and greater efficiency?
2	Does the project enhance the asset value at the lowest construction cost compared to traditional procurement?
3	Has there been a fiscal assessment approved by the Ministry of Finance that ensures funding for direct and indirect liabilities over the project life cycle?
4	Does the project contain a recent demand analysis to avoid over dimensioning the project?
5	Are risks allocated to the party most able to manage or mitigate them?
6	Is the project flexible to accommodate changes in demand and political cycle instability?
7	Does the private sector operator have the capacity to manage risks transferred by the government?
8	Does the contract have provisions to manage disputes that are specific to the type of concession and the sector?
9	Can the public sector handle well the risks that were retained?
10	How capable is the private partner of delivering expected results?
11	Are design, construction, and operation fully integrated?
12	Is the project total value large enough to justify transaction costs?
13	Has the decision to fund the project been approved independently and prior to the decision to procure as a PPP?
14	Does the government have effective policy or procedures for value for money (VFM) assessment?
15	Does the project have measurable and realistic service standards?
16	Does PPP procurement represent the most efficient business model compared to traditional procurement?
17	Is the tender award based on a competitive and transparent procurement process?
18	Has the project been consulted with stakeholders including the private sector, other government entities, and civil society?
19	Are government payments (or penalties) linked to meeting required performance standards by the private partner?
20	Can the government do this on its own at a reasonable price and quality level?
21	Is there institutional capacity in government to structure the project? Can structuring capacity be found in the private sector?
22	Is there institutional capacity in government to supervise the project?
23	Can the project reach commercial and financial close during the current government?
24	Does the government counterpart have the legal mandate to do PPPs and an appropriate PPP policy framework?
25	Is the new technology proposed in a project accessible and affordable to low-income populations ?

Appendix 2: Key Terms

adjusted public sector comparator	Conversion of project costs to account for the risks that the government retains in traditional government procurement, which in a public–private partnership (PPP) would be allocated to the private partner.
budget rule	Ensures that the "investment decision" always precedes the "procurement decision."
competitive neutrality	An adjustment to the costs of a public sector project that has cost advantages or disadvantages compared to a private company undertaking a PPP. For example, the tax liabilities under the two options may be different. These differences should be corrected for in calculating the public sector comparator.
fiscal illusion	Misperception that PPPs create additional fiscal space due to failure to account for direct or contingent liabilities in PPP projects financed by the private sector.
investment decision	Assesses whether the project's objectives will likely result in net economic benefits, regardless of the procurement method (PPP or a public option).
medium-term budget framework	Fiscal arrangements that allow the government to extend the horizon for fiscal policy-making beyond the annual budgetary calendar. It usually covers the preparation, execution, and monitoring of multi-annual budget plans and contains both expenditure and revenue projections as well as the resulting budget balances.
power purchase agreement	This is a contract between buyers and sellers of renewable energy defining the commercial terms for sale and purchase of electricity and other key contractual clauses such as schedule for energy delivery, payment terms, and termination.
procurement decision	An assessment of which delivery method—PPPs or a public option—will more likely ensure that the project objectives will be achieved. While this is the basis of value for money (VFM), it only makes sense if the project is worth investing in in the first place.
public option	Refers to traditional public procurement of an infrastructure project with limited or no risk allocation to the private sector.
public sector comparator	Comparing the chosen PPP option against what the project would look like if delivered through conventional procurement. It considers fiscal costs and compares the options based on a cost–benefit analysis.
raw public sector comparator	Estimates the whole-life baseline costs of the project if the government is implementing the project through a traditional procurement modality.
whole-of-life costing	Also referred to as "life-cycle costs," it refers to placing responsibility for design, construction, ongoing service delivery, operation, maintenance, and refurbishment with one party and incentivizes that party to complete each project function (design, build, operate, maintain) in a way that minimizes total costs.

Appendix 3: Value for Money—Useful Reference Documents

The literature on value for money is extensive. The following are useful reference documents.

Table A3: Reference Documents on Value for Money Guidance for Public–Private Partnership Projects

Reference	Description	Link
ADB. *Realizing the Vision for Strategy 2020: The Transformational Role of Public–Private Partnerships. Public–Private Partnership Operational Plan 2012–2020.*	This document contains an appendix that provides practical guidance on development of the PSC.	https://www.adb.org/sites/default/files/institutional-document/33671/ppp-operational-plan-2012-2020.pdf#:~:text=Implementation%20of%20the%20PPP%20operational%20plan%20will%20be,supporting%20and%20expanding%20PPP%20initiatives%20within%20its%20offices.
World Bank et al. 2017. *Public–Private Partnerships: Reference Guide – Version 3.0* (2017). Washington, DC.	Comprehensive PPP reference guide, a joint product of the World Bank, the ADB the Inter-American Development Bank (IDB), and others. Also provides details on VFM country practice and practical guidance.	https://ppp.worldbank.org/public-private-partnership/library/ppp-reference-guide-3-0.
ADB. *Public–Private Partnership Monitor, 2017;* and updates.	This publication provides business intelligence on the enabling PPP environment and identifies key gaps in the institutional, legal, and regulatory frameworks in Asia and the Pacific.	Public-Private Partnership Monitor Series | Asian Development Bank (adb.org).
United Kingdom, Her Majesty's Treasury. 2011. *Quantitative Assessment User Guide,* London; and (2011) *Value for Money Quantitative Evaluation Spreadsheet.* London.	Provides detailed guidance and a worked example on the quantitative approach to value for money assessment—calculating the public sector comparator and comparing it to the PPP reference model, as well as an Excel spreadsheet tool for carrying out the analysis.	https://library.pppknowledgelab.org/documents/4331.
Grimsey, D. and Lewis, M.K. 2005. Are Public Private Partnerships value for money? Evaluating alternative approaches and comparing academic and practitioner views. *Accounting Forum* 29(4). pp. 345–378.	Describes approaches to assessing value for money in PPPs, and sets out in detail the PSC approach and its pros and cons.	https://library.pppknowledgelab.org/documents/2297.
Organisation for Economic Co-operation and Development. 2008. *Public–Private Partnerships: In Pursuit of Risk Sharing and Value for Money.* Paris.	Chapter 3 on "The Economics of Public–Private Partnership: is PPP the Best Alternative?" describes the determinants of value for money in a PPP, and how it is typically assessed.	https://library.pppknowledgelab.org/documents/2288.

continued on next page

Table A3: continued

Reference	Description	Link
World Bank. 2009. *Toolkit for Public Private Partnerships in Roads and Highways.*	Section on value for money and the PSC describes the logic behind value for money analysis, how the PSC is used, and some of its shortcomings	https://ppiaf.org/documents/2066.
United Kingdom, Her Majesty's Treasury. 2006. *Value for Money Assessment Guidance.* London.	Describes in detail how value for money should be assessed at three stages: assessing overall programs, particular projects, and during procurement. The guidelines take a quantitative and qualitative approach, and include detailed checklists for the latter.	https://webarchive.nationalarchives.gov.uk/20130102211853/http://www.hm-treasury.gov.uk/infrastructure_ppp_VFM.htm.
Leigland, J. 2006. Is the public sector comparator right for developing countries? Appraising public–private projects in infrastructure. *Gridlines, 4.*	Summarizes common criticisms of PSC analysis, and describes whether and how using PSC analysis may make sense in developing country contexts.	https://ppiaf.org/d/2999/download.
Infrastructure Australia. 2008. *National Public–Private Partnership Guidelines: Volume 4: Public Sector Comparator Guidance.* Canberra.	Provides detailed guidance on calculating the public sector comparator and a worked example, including extracts from the Excel model used.	https://www.infrastructure.gov.au/infrastructure/ngpd/files/Volume-4-PSC-Guidance-Dec-2008-FA.pdf.
Colombia, Ministerio de Hacienda y Crédito Público de Colombia. 2010. Nota Técnica: *Comparador Público-Privado para la selección de proyectos APP.* Bogotá.	Introduces the PSC methodology, explains all the analytic steps, and provides a worked example.	https://library.pppknowledgelab.org/documents/4245.
Shugart, C. 2006. *Quantitative Methods for the Preparation, Appraisal, and Management of PPI Projects in Sub-Saharan Africa: Final Report.* Gaborone, Botswana: New Partnership for Africa's Development.	Describes some methodological inconsistencies and challenges with the PSC, focusing on two related issues: what is the appropriate discount rate to use when calculating present values, and how the cost of risk should be taken into account.	https://ppiaf.org/documents/2979.
Grimsey, D. and Lewis, M.K. 2004. Discount debates: Rates, risk, uncertainty, and value for money in PPPs. *Public Infrastructure Bulletin.* 1(3). pp. 1–5.	Describes the implications of the choice of discount rate in comparing PPP and public procurement, and the relationship between discount rates and risk allocation.	http://shaghool.ir/Files/Grimsey,%20Darrin,%20and%20Mervyn%20K.%20Lewis.%202004.%20%E2%80%9CDiscount%20debates%20Rates,%20risk,.pdf.
Gray, S., Hall, J., and Pollard, G. S. 2010. *The Public–Private Partnership Paradox.* Unpublished.	Provides a more theoretically driven discussion of the choice of discount rate for evaluating PPPs, compared with public procurement projects, emphasizing the difference between discounting future cash outflows and inflows.	https://library.pppknowledgelab.org/documents/4270.

continued on next page

Reference	Description	Link
Australia, Partnerships Victoria. 2009. *Annexure 6: Frequently asked questions and common problems in Public Sector Comparator (PSC) development.* Melbourne.	Lists and answers common questions on when and how the PSC should be used, and some methodological questions. Also describes some common problems in developing the PSC.	https://www.dtf.vic.gov.au/sites/default/files/2018-05/Partnerships-Victoria-Requirements-November-2016.pdf.
European PPP Expertise Centre. 2011. *The Non-Financial Benefits of PPPs: A Review of Concepts and Methodology.* Luxembourg.	Describes the shortcomings of standard PSC analysis, which assesses fiscal costs, but does not take into account nonfinancial costs and benefits. Suggests an alternative approach incorporating nonfinancial benefits in the PSC.	https://www.eib.org/attachments/epec/epec_non_financial_benefits_of_ppps_en.pdf.
New Zealand, National Infrastructure Unit. 2009. *Guidance for Public Private Partnerships in New Zealand.* Auckland.	Chapter 5: "Procurement Options" sets out the logic and analysis for assessing whether procuring a project as a PPP is likely to provide value for money. This includes a simple, quantitative cost–benefit comparison of PPP and public procurement.	https://www.interest.co.nz/sites/default/files/NZ%20PPP%20guide.pdf.
Reyes-Tagle, G., ed. 2018. *Bringing PPPs into the Sunlight, Synergies Now and Pitfalls Later.* Inter-American Development Bank.	The perception among many practitioners that public–private partnerships (PPPs) do not carry fiscal consequences is flawed. Bypassing fiscal constraints is not a valid reason to choose a PPP over traditional public investment (TPI). PPPs do not materially reduce fiscal constraints for governments.	https://publications.iadb.org/publications/english/document/Bringing-PPPs-into-the-Sunlight-Synergies-Now-and-Pitfalls-Later.pdf.
International Monetary Fund. 2020. *Mastering the Risky Business of Public–Private Partnerships in Infrastructure.*	This paper provides key aspects of PPP fiscal risk management as well as the advantages and disadvantages of PPPs. It discusses the fiscal illusion that PPPs, when financed by the private sector, are free to the government.	https://www.imf.org/en/Publications/Departmental-Papers-Policy-Papers/Issues/2021/05/10/Mastering-the-Risky-Business-of-Public-Private-Partnerships-in-Infrastructure-50335?cid=em-COM-123-43064.
Engel, E and Galetovic, A. 2020. When and How to use Public–Private Partnerships in Infrastructure: Lessons from the international Experience. *NBER Working Paper.*	This paper looks at the governance of PPPs, which are more complex than traditional public procurement of infrastructure. It recommends improvements to PPPs through use of appropriate risk allocation and avoidance of opportunistic renegotiations.	https://www.nber.org/system/files/working_papers/w26766/w26766.pdf.

ADB = Asian Development Bank, PPP = public–private partnership, PSC = public sector comparator, VFM = value for money.
Source: Authors.

References

Asian Development Bank (ADB). 2012. *Public–Private Partnership Operational Plan 2012–2020.*

———. 2017. *Guidelines for the Economic Analysis of Projects.*

———. 2018. *Value for Money: Guidance Note on Procurement.*

———. 2020. *Thematic Evaluation: ADB Support for Public–Private Partnerships 2009–2019.*

———. 2021. Forthcoming. Operationalizing Quality Infrastructure Investment Principles in DMCs to Promote Sustainable Infrastructure.

———. 2021. Forthcoming. Strengthening Fiscal Governance and Sustainability in Public–Private Partnerships.

———. Forthcoming. PPP Governance and Sustainable Cities: Case Studies and Lesson Learned in the Water Sector.

ADB et al. 2016. The APMG *Public–Private Partnership (PPP) Certification Guide.* Washington, DC: World Bank Group.

Castalia. 2016. *Municipality-Level Public–Private Partnership (PPP) Operational Framework for Chongqing.* Consultant report to ADB: PPP Value for Money Guidance Note.

European Bank for Reconstruction and Development. 2018. *2017/2018 PPP Laws Assessment in the EBRD Region.* London.

Flyvbjerg, B. 2006. From Nobel Prize to Project Management: Getting Risks Right. *Project Management Journal.* 37 (3). pp. 5–15.

Flyvbjerg, B., C. Hon, and W.H. Fok. 2016. *Reference Class Forecasting for Hong Kong's Major Roadworks Projects.* ICE Proceedings, Hong Kong, China.

Global Infrastructure Hub. 2020. InfraCompass.

Government of Viet Nam. 2019. *Government's Report No. 25/BC-CP on the Status of Implementation of PPP Projects in Viet Nam.*

Hyeon, P. 2012. Government Support for PPP Projects in Korea. Presentation at United Nations Economic and Social Commission for Asia and the Pacific (UNESCAP) Conference. Thailand.

International Monetary Fund. 2015. The Macroeconomic Effects of Public Investment: Evidence from Advanced Economies. *IMF Working Paper.*

International Financial Reporting Standards, International Public Sector Accounting Standard 32 https://www.ifac.org/system/files/publications/files/B8%20IPSAS_32.pdf.

Jay-Hyung, K. et al. 2011. *Public–Private Partnership Infrastructure Projects: Case Studies from the Republic of Korea. Volume 1: Institutional Arrangements and Performance.* ADB. Manila.

Kose, M.A. et al. 2020. Caught by a Cresting Debt Wave. Global Waves of Debt: Causes and Consequences. *Finance & Development*. Volume 57. World Bank.

Leigland, J. 2018. Public–Private Partnerships in Developing Countries: The Emerging Evidence-Based Critique. *The World Bank Research Observer*. 33:1. pp. 103–134.

Moseley, M. 2020. *Restoring Confidence in Public–Private Partnerships Reforming Risk Allocation and Creating More Collaborative PPPs*. ADB.

National Audit Office, United Kingdom. 2013. *Review of the VFM assessment process for PFI*. Briefing for the House of Commons Treasury Select Committee.

National Economic Development Authority (NEDA), Philippines. 2019. Unsolicited PPP Proposals Undergo Rigorous, Holistic Review. Media Statement.

Organisation for Economic Co-operation (OECD). 2015. *Towards a Framework for the Governance of Infrastructure.*

Public–Private Infrastructure Advisory Facility. 2013. *Value-for-Money Analysis-Practices and Challenges.* Report from World Bank Global Roundtable, 28 May 2013, Washington, DC.

State Audit Office of Vietnam. 2017. Proceedings of State Audit Office Conference in Ha Noi. Remarks by Truong Hai Yen, deputy head of the SAV. Viet Nam.

Transport Infrastructure Ireland. 2019. *Reference Class Forecasting Guidelines for use in connection with National Roads Projects.*

United Kingdom National Audit Office. 2013. *Review of the VFM assessment process for PFI*. Briefing for the House of Commons Treasury Select Committee.

World Bank. 2022. Private Participation in Infrastructure (PPI).